Creative Ideas
for YARDS & GARDENS™

Edited by Jeanne Stauffer

HOUSE of
WHITE
BIRCHES
PUBLISHERS
SINCE 1947

Woodworking for Women™
Creative Ideas for Yards & Gardens

Editor: Jeanne Stauffer
Associate Editors: Lisa M. Fosnaugh, Rachelle Haughn
Technical Editors: Marla Freeman, Sandi Hauanio, Cindy Reusser
Copy Editor: Michelle Beck

Photography: Tammy Christian, Kelly Heydinger, Christena Green
Photography Stylist: Tammy Nussbaum

Art Director: Brad Snow
Publishing Services Manager: Brenda Gallmeyer
Graphic Arts Supervisor: Ronda Bechinski
Book Design/Graphic Artist: Amy S. Lin
Production Assistant: Marj Morgan
Traffic Coordinator: Sandra Beres
Technical Artist: John Buskirk, Chad Summers

Chief Executive Officer: John Robinson
Publishing Director: David McKee
Book Marketing Director: Craig Scott
Sales Director: John Boggs
Editorial Director: Vivian Rothe
Publishing Services Director: Brenda R. Wendling

Printed in the United States of America
First Printing: 2004
Library of Congress Number: 2003115890
ISBN: 1-931171-66-1

Every effort has been made to ensure the accuracy and completenessof the
instructions in this book. However, we cannot be responsible forhuman error
or for the results when using materials other than thosespecified in the
instructions, or for variations in individual work.

Important Safety Notice: To prevent accidents, read instructions and use all safety
guards on power equipment. Wear safety goggles and headphones to protect yourself.
Do not wear loose clothing when working on power equipment. Due to the variability
of construction materials and skill levels, neither the staff nor the publisher of
Woodworking for Women books assumes any responsibility for any accidents, injuries,
damages or other losses incurred resulting from the material presented in this book.
See page 174 for additional safety tips.

Welcome

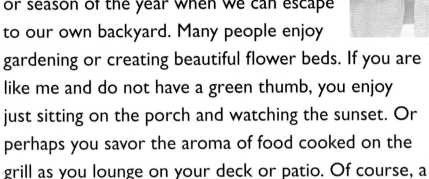

Most of us look forward to the time of day or season of the year when we can escape to our own backyard. Many people enjoy gardening or creating beautiful flower beds. If you are like me and do not have a green thumb, you enjoy just sitting on the porch and watching the sunset. Or perhaps you savor the aroma of food cooked on the grill as you lounge on your deck or patio. Of course, a picnic in your own backyard can't be beat!

Your favorite place may be large and have a great view of the countryside or it may be small, like a balcony patio. In either case, we want to help you make your special place more cozy and inviting with this collection of decorative and functional woodworking projects.

Adding a bench, a flower box or even a fence can make your patio, deck, yard or garden a very special place to be. But don't stop there. Add a tray to help you serve your loved ones, a sign to welcome guests, wind chimes to sway in the breeze or plant labels to decorate your garden. You'll enjoy every minute of the time you spend working with wood and when you are finished, you can relax and enjoy these projects for months and even years, as you relax in your own backyard.

Warm regards,

Jeanne Stauffer

CONTENTS

Porches

Decks & Patios

Yards

Gardens

Porches

PINEAPPLE WELCOME

Design by Cindy Reusser

Pineapples are a sign of hospitality. Use your woodburner to create the pineapple lines and your scroll saw to cut out the shape.

CUTTING

1 Enlarge pattern 172 percent. Transfer outline of pattern to pine board using graphite paper. Cut out using saw.

ASSEMBLE & FINISH

1 Using graphite paper, transfer detail for pineapple and leaves to cutout piece. Working from bottom of pineapple up, go over pineapple and leaf detail with woodburning tool, following manufacturer's directions.

2 Paint leaves dar green; paint pineapple antique gold. Paint bottom portion of sign with cream. Let dry. **Note:** *Do not paint edges of sign.*

3 With red, paint a ⅜-inch-wide border around bottom portion of sign; let dry.

PROJECT SIZE
17x11¼x¾ inches

TOOLS
• Scroll saw, band saw or jigsaw

SUPPLIES
• 18x11¾x¾ pine board
• Fine-grit sandpaper
• Graphite paper
• Woodburning tool
• Acrylic paint: red, dark green, antique gold, black, cream
• Paintbrushes and foam brushes
• Antiquing medium
• Golden oak #210B Wood Finish from MinWax
• Interior/exterior semi-gloss spray polyurethane
• Sawtooth picture hanger

4 Use graphite paper to transfer lettering to bottom portion of sign. Paint lettering with black; let dry.

5 Sand edges lightly. Apply wood finish to entire piece, front and back; wipe off excess. Let dry.

6 Following manufacturer's directions, apply antiquing medium to painted areas, allowing medium to flow into burned lines.

7 Spray entire sign with interior/exterior semi-gloss polyurethane, following manufacturer's directions. Let dry.

8 Attach sawtooth hanger to back of sign. ✸

Pineapple Welcome
Enlarge pattern 172%

WELCOME

WELCOME
PLAQUE

Design by Cindy Reusser

Guests will feel right at home when they step on your porch and see this classic welcome sign. If you don't like to paint letters, just purchase some at your local hardware store.

CUTTING

1 Use graphite paper to transfer end pattern to both ends of pine board and mark hole placement. Cut out. Drill holes.

2 Sand edges smooth.

FINISH

1 Base-coat plaque with black; let dry. Top-coat plaque with dark red; let dry.

2 Enlarge lettering 165 percent. Transfer to plaque using graphite paper. Paint with cream; let dry.

3 Lightly sand entire piece to reveal some of black undercoat and create an aged appearance.

4 Apply antiquing medium following manufacturer's directions.

5 Spray entire plaque with interior/exterior semi-gloss polyurethane, following manufacturer's directions. Let dry. ✺

PROJECT SIZE
3½x19¼x¾ inches

TOOLS
• Scroll saw or jigsaw
• Drill with ⅜-inch bit

SUPPLIES
• 20x3½x¾-inch pine board
• Graphite paper
• Fine-grit sandpaper
• Acrylic painta: dark red, black, cream
• Paintbrushes and foam brushes
• Antiquing medium
• Interior/exterior semi-gloss spray
   polyurethane

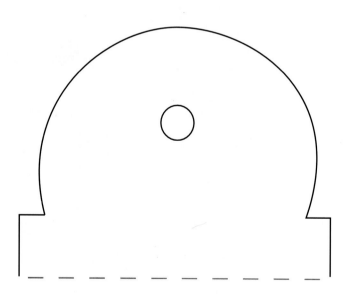

**Welcome Plaque
End**

**W
E
L
C
O
M
E**

**Welcome Plaque
Lettering**
Enlarge 165%

TILE TABLETOP

Design by Lisa Marto Weber

Give an old table new life with this tile tabletop that is reminiscent of your last trip to the ocean. The tabletop fits easily over an existing table, or sturdy legs can be added to make a brand-new table.

CUTTING

1 Cut 1x4 into two 22-inch lengths and two 23½-inch lengths for sides.

2 Beginning and ending 1–2 inches from each end, drill three pilot holes evenly spaced on each side ¾ inches from one long edge.

3 With ⅞-inch bit, drill each hole ¼-inch deep for inserting plugs.

4 Using tile cutter, cut each 4-inch white ceramic tile in half diagonally.

ASSEMBLE & FINISH

1 Glue and screw sides to plywood. **Note:** *sides should extend approximately ¼ inch above plywood.* Sand smooth. Paint with white satin acrylic enamel; let dry.

2 Using tile adhesive, glue 12-inch-square ceramic tile in center of plywood. Referring to photo, glue half tiles between center tile and table edges; glue pebbles between tiles and around outer edge. Let dry 12 hours.

3 Following manufacturer's directions, mix grout and apply to table top using float at a 45-degree angle. Let dry 15 minutes.

4 Wipe grout film from tiles and pebbles using sponge and a basin of water. **Note:** *Do not rinse grout down sink drain.* Let dry.

5 Apply grout sealer; let dry. ❀

PROJECT SIZE
Outer dimensions: 23½x23½x3¾ inches
Inner dimensions: 22x22x2½ inches

TOOLS
- Table saw or hand saw
- Drill with bit to fit screws and ⅞-inch bit
- Tile cutter

SUPPLIES
- 1x4: 8 feet pine
- 22x22x¾-inch plywood
- ⅞-inch wooden button plugs
- 12 wood screws
- Wood glue
- Sandpaper
- White satin acrylic enamel
- 1-inch flat paintbrush
- 12-inch-square ceramic tile
- Eight 4-inch-square white ceramic tiles
- Approximately 100 each blue and pink glass pebbles
- Tile adhesive
- Antique white sanded grout
- Float
- Sponge
- Basin of water
- Grout sealer

Underside of tabletop.

BIRDHOUSE
PEG RACK

Design by Cindy Reusser

Hang your drying herbs, hat or gardening tools in style right on your porch. Pegs can be purchased ready-made or you can turn them. It's your choice!

CUTTING

1 Enlarge pattern pieces 165 percent; join along center dashed line. Using graphite paper and pencil, transfer outline of birdhouse design onto pine board.

2 Set rip fence on table saw 3 inches from blade; set blade height at ⅛ inch. Cut groove at bottom of birdhouse.

3 With scroll saw, cut on traced lines; lightly sand edges.

4 Use pencil to mark locations of holes, perches and pegs. Drill birdhouse holes 1 inch in diameter and ⅜ inch deep; drill holes for perches ¼ inch in diameter and ¼ inch deep; drill holes for pegs ½ inch in diameter and ½ inch deep.

5 With straight-edge ruler and woodburning tool, mark lines between birdhouses.

PAINTING

1 With black, base-coat entire project, including Shaker pegs and perches; let dry.

2 Paint birdhouses antique gold. Paint Shaker pegs, perches and peg rack portion dark red. Let dry.

3 Lightly sand all edges to create a worn look. Following manufacturer's directions, apply antiquing medium to entire project; buff to desired shade.

ASSEMBLE & FINISH

1 Glue perches and pegs into drilled holes. Attach stars with

---

PROJECT SIZE
10¾x24x¾ inches

TOOLS
- Table saw
- Scroll saw
- Drill with 1-inch, ½-inch and ¼-inch bits

SUPPLIES
- 24x11½x¾-inch pine board
- Graphite paper
- Pencil
- Fine-grit sand paper
- Straight-edge ruler
- Woodburning tool
- Acrylic paint: black, antique gold and dark red
- 3 (3⅜x⅞-inch) Shaker pegs with ½-inch tenons
- 6 (1-inch) lengths ¼-inch wooden dowels (for perches)
- Antiquing medium
- Wood glue
- 3 (1½-inch) rusty stars
- Small brad nails
- 2 (½-inch) brass picture hangers
- Interior/exterior semi-gloss spray polyurethane

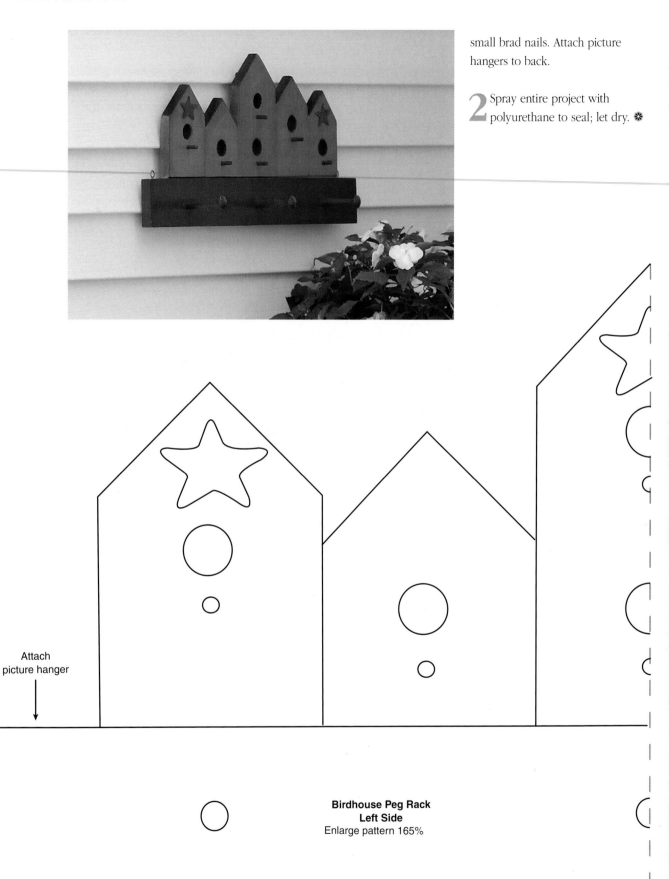

small brad nails. Attach picture hangers to back.

2 Spray entire project with polyurethane to seal; let dry. ❈

Attach
picture hanger

Birdhouse Peg Rack
Left Side
Enlarge pattern 165%

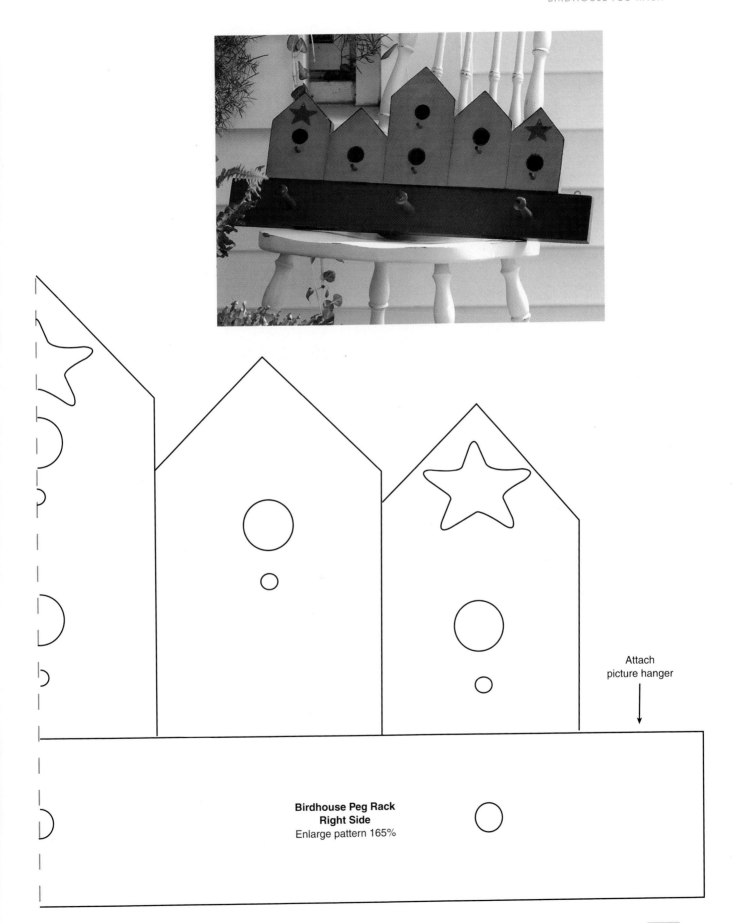

Attach
picture hanger

**Birdhouse Peg Rack
Right Side**
Enlarge pattern 165%

PORCH RAILING SHELF

Design by Barbara Greve

PROJECT SIZE
20½x7¾x7¾ inches

SUPPLIES
- 21½x7¾x½-inch pine or plywood board
- 20½x1⅝x¼-inch poplar or pine board
- Five 7½x1½-inch railing spindles
- Two 7¾x7¾-inch railing brackets
- Fine-grit sandpaper
- Paper towels
- Wood glue
- Ten 1-inch brads
- Eight ¾-inch brads
- ¹⁄₃₂-inch nail set
- Wood putty
- All-purpose sealer
- Acrylic paints: white, burnt umber, brown
- Matte varnish

Add this quick, stylish shelf to your porch. The decorative brackets at each end of the shelf can be purchased ready-made at your local home-improvement or hardware store.

INSTRUCTIONS

1 Sand rough parts on wooden pieces smooth; remove dust with damp paper towel.

2 Mark 2 inches from each side of ½-inch-thick board on one edge; mark placement for a 1½-inch railing spindle inside each 2-inch mark. Mark placement of three additional 1½-inch spindles evenly spaced across same edge of board between end spindle marks.

3 Glue ends of spindles in spaces marked and let dry; pound 1-inch brads through board into each spindle center to secure.

4 Glue top of one railing bracket on each end of ½-inch-thick board, positioning so tops of brackets are flush with edges of board; let dry. Pound three ¾-inch brads evenly spaced through board into top of each railing bracket.

5 Glue ¼-inch-thick board to opposite ends of spindles and bottom inside edges of railing brackets and let dry; pound a ¾-inch brad through each corner bracket into ¼-inch board to secure.

6 Using nail set, countersink brads into shelf; fill holes with wood putty and sand smooth following manufacturer's directions.

7 Apply all-purpose sealer to shelf; let dry. Sand smooth; remove dust with damp paper towel. Mix two parts burnt umber with one part brown; base-coat shelf. Let dry two hours.

8 Paint over base coat with white; let dry to the touch. Sand lightly to create distressed look.

9 Apply two coats of varnish following manufacturer's directions. ✿

BENCH PLANTER

Design by Lisa Marto Weber

Add a cute mini bench to your porch that is just big enough to hold small pots of flowers. The dry-brush painting technique gives this bench a marbled look.

CUTTING

1 Enlarge pattern for bench ends 155 percent. Using scroll saw and enlarged pattern, cut one bench end from each 15-inch 1x12.

2 Enlarge pattern for heart back 105 percent. Trace enlarged pattern onto paper; flip pattern at center line and trace again to create a symmetrical pattern 20 inches long. Using scroll saw and enlarged pattern, cut heart back from 21-inch 1x4.

3 Using jigsaw, measure and cut 1x6 cedar board into a 19-inch length (A); cut each 1x2 furring strip into a 19-inch length (B) for slats.

4 For bench top, draw two 4 ¼-inch circles approximately 3 inches apart in center of 19-inch 1x6 (A). Drill a ½-inch pilot hole in center of each circle, then cut out with jigsaw.

5 Sand all rough edges; remove dust with tack cloth.

ASSEMBLE & FINISH

1 Referring to assembly diagram, apply wood glue to top of bench ends; press bench top (A) into place and let dry. Nail in place with nail gun or finish nails. Attach slats (B) and heart back in same manner.

2 Fill nail holes with wood putty and sand following manufacturer's directions.

3 Using 1-inch paintbrush, base-coat bench with white; let dry. Dry-brush white bench with colonial blue; let dry. Paint outsides of flowerpots in same manner, but using colonial blue for base coat and white for dry brushing.

4 Fill flowerpots as desired and place in holes in bench top. ✽

PROJECT SIZE
20x10x13¾ inches

TOOLS
- Scroll saw
- Jigsaw
- Drill with ½-inch bit
- Nail gun with 1½-inch nails, or finish nails

SUPPLIES
- 1x12: two 15-inch lengths pine
- 1x6: one 20-inch length cedar
- 1x4: one 21-inch length pine
- 1x2 pine furring strips: 7 feet
- Sandpaper
- Tack cloth
- Multi-task wood glue
- Wood putty
- Americana satin enamel from DecoArt:
  colonial blue #DSA18, white satin
  #DSA01
- 1-inch flat wash paintbrush
- Two 4¼-inch terra-cotta flower pots

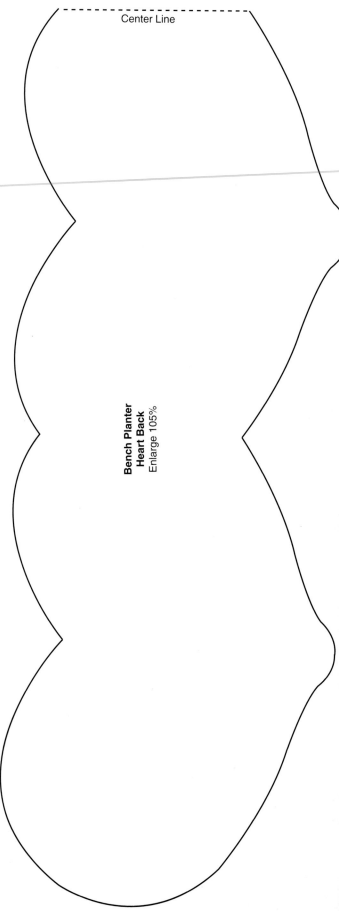

Center Line

Bench Planter
Heart Back
Enlarge 105%

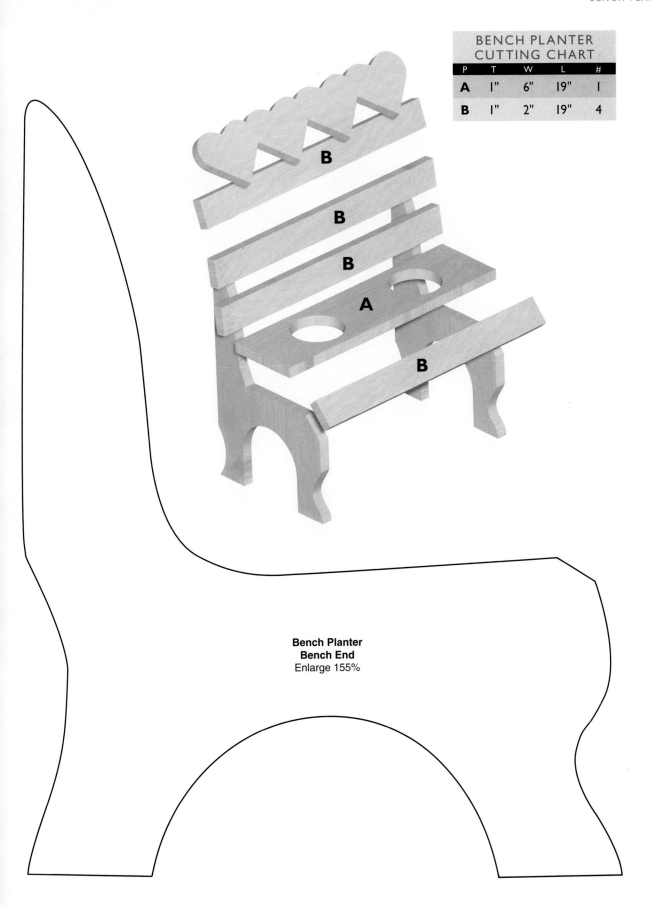

BENCH PLANTER
CUTTING CHART

P	T	W	L	#
A	1"	6"	19"	1
B	1"	2"	19"	4

Bench Planter
Bench End
Enlarge 155%

MAILBOX

Design by Cindy Reusser

The simple lines of this classic mailbox will fit on the porch of any home. As always, a project made with wood adds a touch of warmth.

CUTTING

1 Enlarge patterns for back top and bottom edges 130 percent. Trace enlarged pattern for top edge onto top of 20¼-length 1x12 (C), marking hole placement. Trace pattern for bottom edge onto bottom of same piece. Use scroll saw or jigsaw to cut on trace lines; drill ⅜-inch hole.

2 For front, set table saw blade to a 25-degree angle. Crosscut one end of 10-inch 1x12 (B) to yield an overall length of 9¾ inches.

3 For lid, cutting with the grain of wood, rip cut the 12-inch 1x8 (D) at same 25-degree angle. Return table saw blade to normal position; trim 1x8 lid to a length ³⁄₁₆ inches longer than width of 1x12 front and back pieces.

4 For sides, use table saw to rip cut 34-inch 1x6 (A) to a 4-inch width; cut two 11½-inch lengths from this piece. **Note:** *Save remaining 4-inch-wide length to use in step 2 of assembly. Set miter attachment on table saw to 25 degrees; cut one end of each piece.*

5 Sand all pieces smooth.

ASSEMBLE & FINISH

1 Place both side pieces (A) on edge on a flat surface with longest angled side down. Using glue and nails, attach front piece (B) to sides.

2 Glue and nail back (C) to opposite side edges. Measure opening in bottom of mailbox; cut remaining 4-inch-wide length to that measurement; glue and nail into place.

3 Fill and sand nail holes with wood putty, following manufacturer's directions.

4 Remove all sanding residue with tack cloth. Finish inside and outside of mailbox and lid with exterior paint or stain following manufacturer's direction; let dry.

5 Attach hinges with screws to lid (D) and back (A) approximately 1½ inches from each side.

6 Attach mailbox to wall or post in covered location for best protection from the elements. ❀

MAILBOX CUTTING CHART

P	T	W	L	#
A	1"	6"	34"	1
B	1"	12"	10"	1
C	1"	12"	20¼"	1
D	1"	8"	12"	1

PROJECT SIZE
11x20x5½ inches

TOOLS
- Scroll saw or jigsaw
- Drill with ⅜-inch bit
- Table saw with miter edge
- Phillips head screwdriver
- Nail gun with 2-inch nails or hammer and 2-inch finish nails

SUPPLIES
- Stock pine 1x12: one 20¼ inches; one 10 inches
- Stock pine 1x8: 12 inches
- Stock pine 1x6: 34 inches
- Medium-grit sandpaper
- Exterior wood glue
- Wood putty
- Putty knife
- Tack cloth
- Exterior paint or stain
- 2-inch paintbrush
- One pair 2½-inch non-mortising hinges with screws

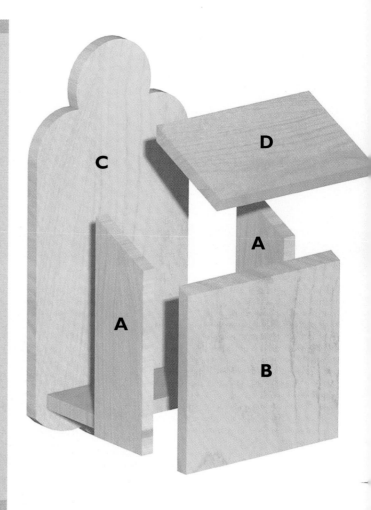

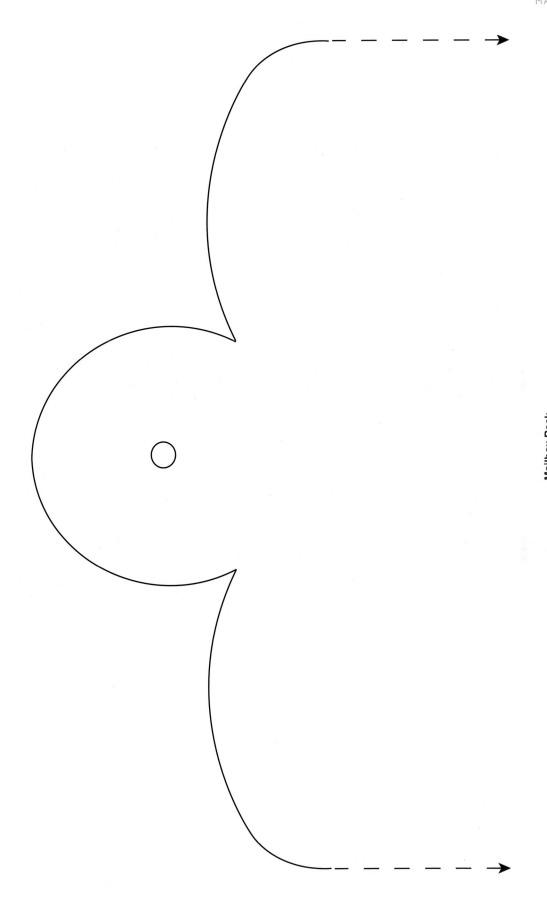

Mailbox Back
Top Edge
Enlarge pattern 130%

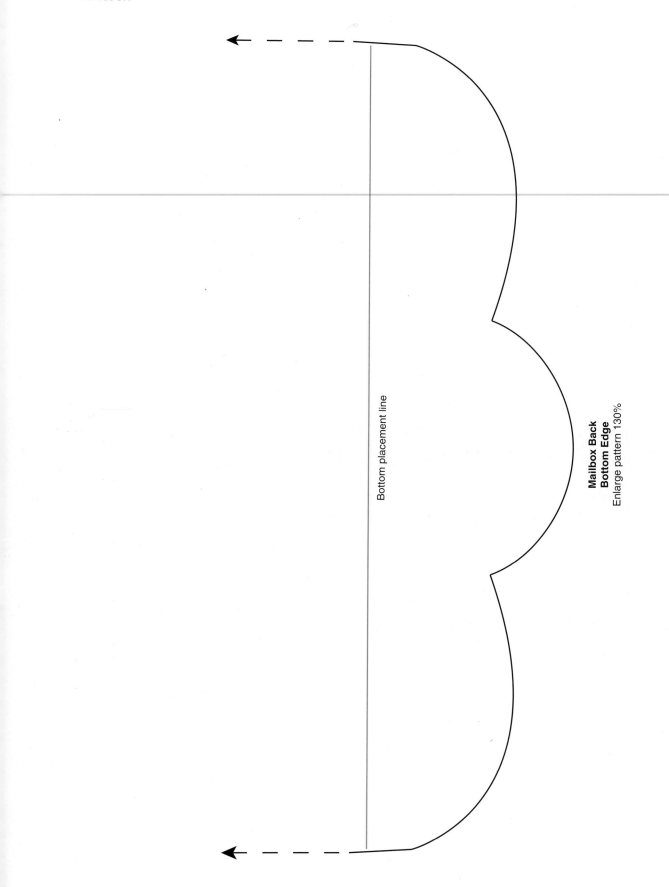

Bottom placement line

Mailbox Back
Bottom Edge
Enlarge pattern 130%

WOOD & COPPER WIND CHIMES

Design by Barbara Matthiessen

Wood and copper pipes combine for an elegant and pleasant-sounding wind chime. To better secure the knots in the nylon cord, melt the ends with a kitchen match.

PROJECT NOTE

When attaching chimes to base, ends of nylon cord can be melted with a kitchen match to secure knots.

BASE

1 Glue 4-inch plaque on top of 5-inch plaque. Let glue set; sand edges and wipe with tack cloth.

2 Stain plaques following manufacturer's directions; let dry. Paint lines on finial and edge of top plaque with gold metallic paint; let dry.

3 On bottom of 5-inch plaque mark center; mark 1 inch from center on opposite sides, and 1½ inches in from each corner. Use awl to make a hole at each mark for starting screw; attach ⅝-inch eye screws.

4 Mark center top of top plaque; make a starter hole with nail punch, then attach finial. Make a starter hole in top of finial with awl; attach 1⅛-inch eye screw.

5 Following manufacturer's directions, apply two coats of varnish to wooden plaques, letting dry after each coat.

CHIMES

1 Using 1/16-inch bit, drill a hole through center of 2½-inch wooden star; drill another hole through one point on 3-inch wooden star. Paint with gold metallic paint; let dry.

2 Use pipe cutter to cut copper piping into 15¼-, 13-, 12-, 11¼-, 10- and 7-inch lengths for chimes. On each length, use nail punch to make a dent ¾ inch from one end; use 1/32-inch bit, drill hole straight through both sides of pipe. Run metal file inside pipes over drilled holes and across ends to remove any rough edges or metal bits. If desired, lightly sand to remove any markings. *Note: Copper pipe will rapidly acquire a natural verdigris finish.*

3 Clip snap swivel onto eye screw on finial; attach a 10- to 20-inch length of utility cord to snap swivel with a lark's head knot. Tie ends with a double overhand knot.

4 Thread a 14- to 20-inch length of utility cord through holes on each copper pipe, pulling ends even; tie an overhand knot just above top of pipe. Tie ends of cords to six outer 5/8-inch eye screws with a single knot. Hang to test for balance; adjust as necessary then tie permanent overhand knots.

5 Cut a 32-inch length of cord. Thread 3-inch star to center of cord, then tie an overhand knot right above star; skip approximately 3 inches of cording, then make a double overhand knot. Thread on 2½-inch star; tie an overhand knot right above star. Attach ends of cord to center eye screw with a double overhand knot. ✿

PROJECT SIZE
5x33x5 inches

TOOLS
- Awl
- Nail punch
- Drill with 1/16- and 1/32-inch bits
- Pipe cutter
- Fine metal file

SUPPLIES
- 5x5x¾-inch wood plaque with routed edge
- 4x4x¾-inch wood plaque with routed edge
- Wood glue
- Medium- to fine-grit sandpaper
- Tack cloth
- Wooden drapery-rod finial
- Acrylic stain or paint to match finial
- Gold metallic paint
- Paintbrush
- Eye screws: one 1⅛-inch, seven 5/8-inch
- Exterior varnish
- Precut wooden stars: 3 inches and 2½ inches
- 6 feet ½-inch copper pipe
- One snap swivel
- Black nylon utility cord

SMALL WOOD BOX

Design by Barbara Greve

Purchased door frame squares create two projects in one: a candle stand and a small box.

INSTRUCTIONS

1 Sand wood pieces smooth; remove dust with a damp paper towel.

2 Using photo and diagram as a guide, form box from door frame squares; glue in place. Let dry.

3 Glue ¼-inch wood rectangle on bottom of box; let dry.

4 Hammer brads through bottom of box into sides, as shown in diagram. Countersink nails with nail set. Following manufacturer's directions, fill holes with wood putty and sand.

5 Apply a coat of all-purpose sealer to box; let dry. Sand lightly if needed.

6 Base-coat box with burnt umber; let dry a few hours. Cover burnt umber with white, applying as many coats as needed to cover entirely; let dry.

7 Sand lightly to randomly expose burnt umber, creating a distressed look.

8 Following manufacturer's directions, apply two coats of varnish, letting dry after each coat. ✺

PROJECT SIZE
5¾x3¾x4 inches

SUPPLIES
- Four 3¾x3¾-inch door frame squares
- 5¼x3¾x¼-inch wood stock
- Fine-grit sandpaper
- Damp paper towel
- Thick white craft glue
- ¾-inch brads
- 1/32-inch nail set
- Wood putty
- All-purpose sealer
- Ceramcoat acrylic paint from Delta: white #2525 and burnt umber #2025
- Matte varnish

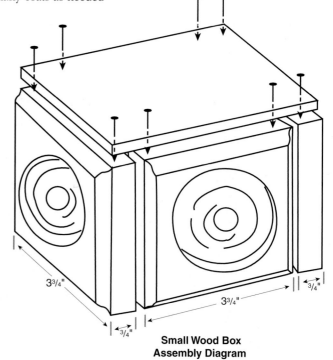

3¾"

3¾"

3/4"

3/4"

**Small Wood Box
Assembly Diagram**

Decks & Patios

FIREWOOD BOX

Design by Johanna Johanson

The hand-cut dovetails make this a project for an intermediate or experienced woodworker. The box is made with a removable plywood bottom that can easily be replaced.

PROJECT NOTE
Box is made with a removable plywood bottom that sits on four cleats so that it can be replaced if the plywood becomes unsound due to damp firewood.

CUTTING

1 Using table saw, cut 1x8 into four 24$\frac{1}{16}$-inch lengths and four 16$\frac{1}{16}$-inch lengths. **Note:** *Additional $\frac{1}{16}$-inch length will make dovetails a bit proud.* Rip cut precise width and thickness of two 24-inch lengths to 7$\frac{1}{2}$x$\frac{3}{4}$ inches (A), two 24-inch lengths to 7x$\frac{3}{4}$ inches (B), two 16-inch lengths to 7$\frac{1}{2}$x$\frac{3}{4}$ inches (C) and two 16-inch lengths to 7x$\frac{3}{4}$ inches (D). Cut 1x1 into two 22-inch lengths (E) and two 13-inch lengths (F); set aside for cleats.

2 Referring to cutting diagram, cut 1-inch-deep notches on bottoms of 7$\frac{1}{2}$-inch-wide boards, beginning pattern 2 inches in from each end.

3 Lay out all four panels, making sure edges of top and bottom panels fit together precisely. **Note:** *If adjustment is needed, rejoint all eight pieces to maintain consistency.*

4 Using pattern provided, cut triangle for Maltese cross onto heavy cardboard; draw line from center of baseline to point of triangle.

5 Attach front bottom panel (A) to front top panel (B) with three or four 2-inch pieces of double-sided tape, making sure edges and ends of boards are flush. Repeat for back panels.

6 Mark center on each set of front and back panels; place point of triangle at this point and trace pattern onto top panel. Trace again onto bottom panel, with point of triangle at same center point. Centering triangle at same point, trace pattern on each side of first two triangles, aligning center line on triangle with joined edges of panels. Mark center points for two more crosses 6 inches on each side of center point of first cross; beginning at these points, trace as for first cross. Separate panels and remove tape. Cut out crosses using band saw, jigsaw or Japanese saw.

7 Repeat steps 5 and 6 for end panels (C and D), tracing crosses 3 inches on each side of center of panels.

8 Glue top and bottom panels together for front, back and each end, taking care they match and are level; clamp. Wipe off excess glue; let dry.

9 Cut the dovetails. Since more stress will be on the sides of the box, cut the pins on the sides and the tails on the ends. **Note:** *The design shows three groups of dovetails unevenly spaced, which has more visual interest.*

PROJECT SIZE
24x16x14½ inches

TOOLS
- Table saw
- Band saw, jigsaw or Japanese saw
- Drill with countersink attachment
- Jointer (optional)

SUPPLIES
- 1x8: two 8-foot lengths
- 1x1: one 6-ft length
- One 22½x14½-inch piece of ½-inch plywood
- Heavy cardboard
- Double-sided tape
- Exterior wood glue
- 8 to 10 clamps
- Ten 1-inch wood screws
- Wax paper
- Sandpaper
- Tack cloth
- Desired paint or stain

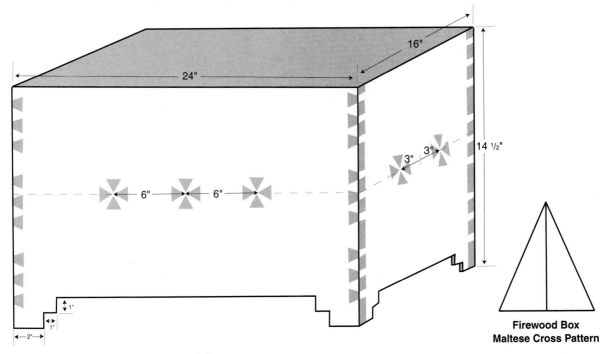

**Firewood Box
Cutting Diagram**

**Firewood Box
Maltese Cross Pattern**

FIREWOOD BOX CUTTING CHART

P	T	W	L	#
A	¾"	7½"	24"	2
B	¾"	7"	24"	2
C	¾"	7½"	16"	2
D	¾"	7"	16"	2
E	1"	1"	22"	2
F	1"	1"	13"	2

ASSEMBLE & FINISH

1 Dry assemble box. Trim plywood for box bottom so it slides into box without being forced, and without a gap of more than ¹⁄₁₆ inch on all sides. **Note:** *Bottom will be used during glue-up to keep the box square.*

2 Position cleats (E and F) inside box to assure proper fit; trim if necessary. Glue cleats to sides and ends of box, having bottom of each cleat level with the tops of cutout notches. Reinforce attachment of cleats with three 1-inch screws on each front and back panel and two 1-inch screws on each end panel.

3 Disassemble box; apply glue to dovetails and reassemble. Slip plywood bottom inside box, using wax paper at corners to protect plywood from glue squeeze-out. Let dry.

4 Sand or chisel dovetails so they are flush with the sides.

5 Sand box; wipe with tack cloth. Finish as desired. ✿

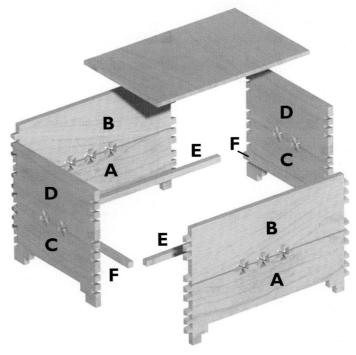

GRILL CART

Design by Barbara Matthiessen

A ready-made cabinet offers design flexibility.

PROJECT NOTES

Use square to mark all cuts. Predrilling holes will prevent wood from splitting.

CART BASE

1 Assemble cabinet base according to manufacturer's directions.

2 Cut 5-foot 2x4 into two pieces to fit inside width of bottom of base for caster supports; position across front and back of inside bottom of base, leaving space between each 2x4 and cabinet for casters to swivel. Attach with 2-inch galvanized screws and glue. Do not over tighten.

3 Position casters on 2x4 supports at corners of cabinet; mark and predrill holes with the $3/32$-inch drill bit. Attach casters with ¼x1-inch lag screws.

4 Enlarge pattern for side bracket 118 percent. Use graphite paper to transfer enlarged pattern onto 12x18x1-inch pine board to make two side brackets. Cut out using scroll saw or jigsaw. Mark placement of hole on each bracket; drill ½-inch deep using 1-inch bit.

5 Cut the 1-inch dowel to fit width of cabinet between brackets. Mark position of brackets on left side of cabinet; predrill two holes per bracket using ¼-inch bit.

6 Sand side brackets and dowel. Apply exterior primer and paint following manufacturer's directions; let dry.

7 Attach shelf bracket to cabinet from the inside using the 2-inch wood screws and glue.

8 Using #6 pilot bit, predrill holes around all four sides of 30x21½x½-inch AC plywood, ⅜-inch

from edge and 3 to 4 inches apart. Attach plywood to cabinet top using ¾-inch #6 screws and glue.

9 Apply exterior primer and paint to 30x33x⅛-inch hardboard. Using ¹⁄₆₄-inch drill bit, predrill holes around peremiter, ⅜ inch from edge and 4 to 5 inches apart. Attach to back of cabinet using brass brads or finish nails and glue.

CART TOP

1 Find the vertical and horizontal center of the plywood top. Following manufacturer's directions, adhere ceramic tiles to top in six rows of four tiles each; let dry.

2 Fill screw holes in plywood top with putty and sand following manufacturer's directions. Apply exterior primer and paint to exposed edges of top; let dry.

3 Cut oak trim molding into two 30-inch lengths (A) for front and back trim, and two 17⅜-inch lengths (B) for side trim. Carefully measure width of top on each side between tiles and edge of top; use table saw to cut trim pieces to exact widths needed.

4 Stain oak strips and seal with clear exterior varnish following manufacturer's directions; let dry. Nail strips around tiles using 1-inch finish nails and glue (Fig. 1); fill nail holes with tinted wood putty.

5 Mask oak strips with painters' tape. Carefully grout tiles following manufacturer's directions.

LATTICE

1 Cut cedar 1x2s into two 30-inch lengths (C), two 27-inch lengths (D) and two 57-inch lengths (E).

PROJECT SIZE
37¾x22½x61¾ inches, excluding castors

TOOLS
- Power saw or handsaw
- Scroll saw or jigsaw
- Table saw or band saw
- Drill with ³⁄₃₂-, ¹⁄₆₄-, ¼- and 1-inch bits, and #6 pilot bit
- Square
- Phillips head screwdriver

SUPPLIES
- Pine 2x4: one 5-foot length*
- AC plywood: 30x21½x½-inches*
- 10-foot length ¼-inch-thick oak trim molding at least 2⅛ inches wide*
- Cedar 1x2s: four 5-foot lengths*
- Hardboard or paneling: 30x33x1/8-inches*
- Finished cabinet base 30 inches wide x 33 inches high x 21½ inches deep
- 2-inch galvanized wood screws
- Wood glue
- Four 2½-inch heavy-duty swivel casters
- ¼x1-inch lag screws: 16
- Graphite paper

- 12x18x1-inch pine board
- 1-inch hardwood dowel: 20 inches
- Sandpaper
- Exterior primer and paint
- Paintbrush
- ¾-inch #6 screws
- ⅝-inch #18 brass brads
- 1-inch finish nails
- 4-inch-square ceramic tiles: 24
- Premixed, nonsanded white ceramic tile adhesive and grout
- Disposable latex gloves, tile adhesive trowel and tile grout sponge floater
- Wood putty
- Golden oak stain
- Clear exterior varnish
- Tinted wood putty to match stain
- 2-inch-wide painters' tape
- Plastic lattice: 30x30-inches*
- 1¼-inch galvanized wood screws
- Barbecue utensils
- Large S hooks

*Cabinet dimensions may vary; adjust measurements accordingly to fit.

2 Sand smooth. Apply exterior primer and paint following manufacturer's directions; let dry.

3 Referring to Fig. 2, place (C) strips and (D) strips on flat surface, best side down, for lattice frame. Position plastic lattice over frame. Using $1/64$-inch bit, predrill holes through lattice only; attach lattice to frame with brass brads.

4 On back of lattice, position (E) strips on sides of frame with top edges even. Predrill using $3/32$-inch bit; attach strips to lattice using $1\frac{1}{4}$-inch galvanized wood screws.

5 To attach lattice frame to cabinet, predrill extended portions of (E)

strips every 3 to 4 inches using $3/32$-inch bit. Attach lattice frame to back of cabinet using 2-inch galvanized wood screws and glue.

6 Hang barbecue utensils on lattice with large S hooks. ❀

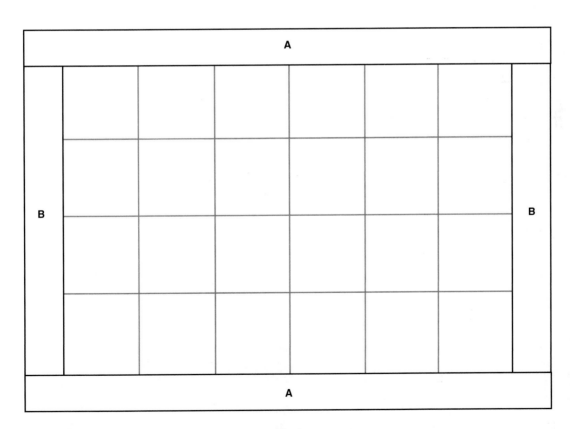

Fig. 1
Grill Cart Top

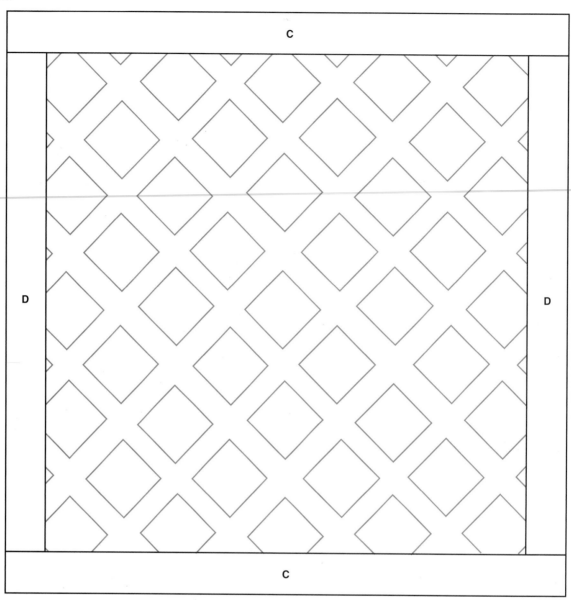

Fig. 2
Grill Cart Lattice Frame

Creative Ideas for Yards & Gardens

The towel rod on this grill cart is only for decoration or hanging towels. If you want to use the handle to move the grill cart from one place to another, you will need to make the brackets stronger, so they don't break. Make towel brackets stronger by using a hardwood such as oak or maple for each bracket. Attach dowel to brackets by pre-drilling and using a lag screw to attach the dowel to each bracket.

GRILL CART CUTTING CHART

P	T	W	L	#
A	¼"	2⅛"	30"	2
B	¼"	2⅛"	17⅜"	2
C	1"	2"	30"	2
D	1"	2"	27"	2
E	1"	2"	57"	2

Grill Cart
Side Bracket
Enlarge pattern 118%

STORAGE BENCH

Design by Bev Shenefield

A purchased or sewn cushion adds versatility to this unique piece. Use it to store your gardening tools or outdoor barbecue picnic supplies.

CUTTING

1 Cut 2x4s into four 33-inch lengths (C), four 20-inch lengths (B), four 17-inch lengths (A) and two 13-inch lengths (D).

2 Cut 2x2 into three 20-inch lengths (E).

3 Cut 1x6s into fourteen 36-inch lengths (F), eight 26-inch lengths (G) and six 20-inch lengths (H).

4 Mark center top of one 26-inch 1x6 (G). On left side of board, mark 3 inches from top; use square to mark corresponding measurement on right side of board. Draw a line from left mark to center, and from right mark to center. Cut on lines for picket. Using this board as a pattern, mark and cut remaining seven 26-inch 1x6s (G) and six 36-inch 1x6s for pickets (F).

5 Referring to bench bottom assembly diagram, make 3½-inch-wide by 1½-inch-deep notches at corners and centers of two 36-inch 1x6s (F).

ASSEMBLE & FINISH

1 Assemble frame according to diagram using screws and exterior wood glue. Check frequently that all parts are square.

2 Nail notched 36-inch 1x6s and two additional 36-inch 1x6s (F) to bottom of frame (see assembly diagram and photo).

3 Referring to lid assembly diagram, nail three 20-inch 2x2s (E) across remaining four 36-inch 1x6s (F). If desired, attach lid to frame with hinges and hasp. ***Note:** 2x2s are on bottom of lid.*

4 Nail six 36-inch pickets (F) across back of frame; nail four 26-inch pickets (G) across each end of frame; nail six 20-inch 1x6s (H) across front (see photo).

5 If desired, attach casters to the bottom of frame (see photo).

6 Apply exterior paint or stain to all surfaces of bench, following manufacturer's directions. ❀

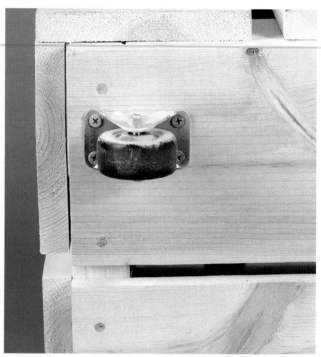

PROJECT SIZE
37½x25½x36 inches

TOOLS
- Handsaw or power saw
- Square

SUPPLIES
- 2x4s: four 10-foot lengths pine or cedar
- 2x2s: one 6-foot length pine or cedar
- 1x6s: twelve 6-foot lengths pine or cedar
- 3-inch galvanized wood screws
- Exterior wood glue
- 7D galvanized nails
- Hinges and hasp (optional)
- 4 heavy-duty casters (optional)
- Exterior paint or stain

STORAGE BENCH CUTTING CHART

P	T	W	L	#
A	2"	4"	17"	4
B	2"	4"	20"	4
C	2"	4"	33"	4
D	2"	4"	13"	2
E	2"	2"	20"	3
F	1"	6"	36"	14
G	1"	6"	26"	8
H	1"	6"	20"	6

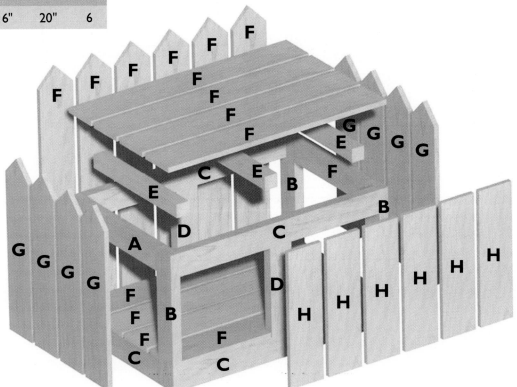

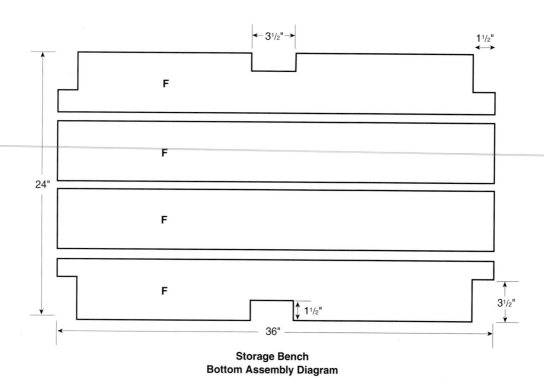

**Storage Bench
Bottom Assembly Diagram**

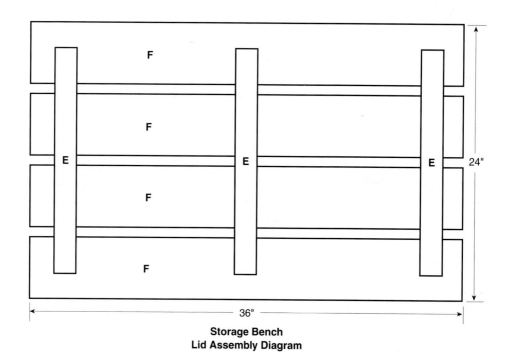

**Storage Bench
Lid Assembly Diagram**

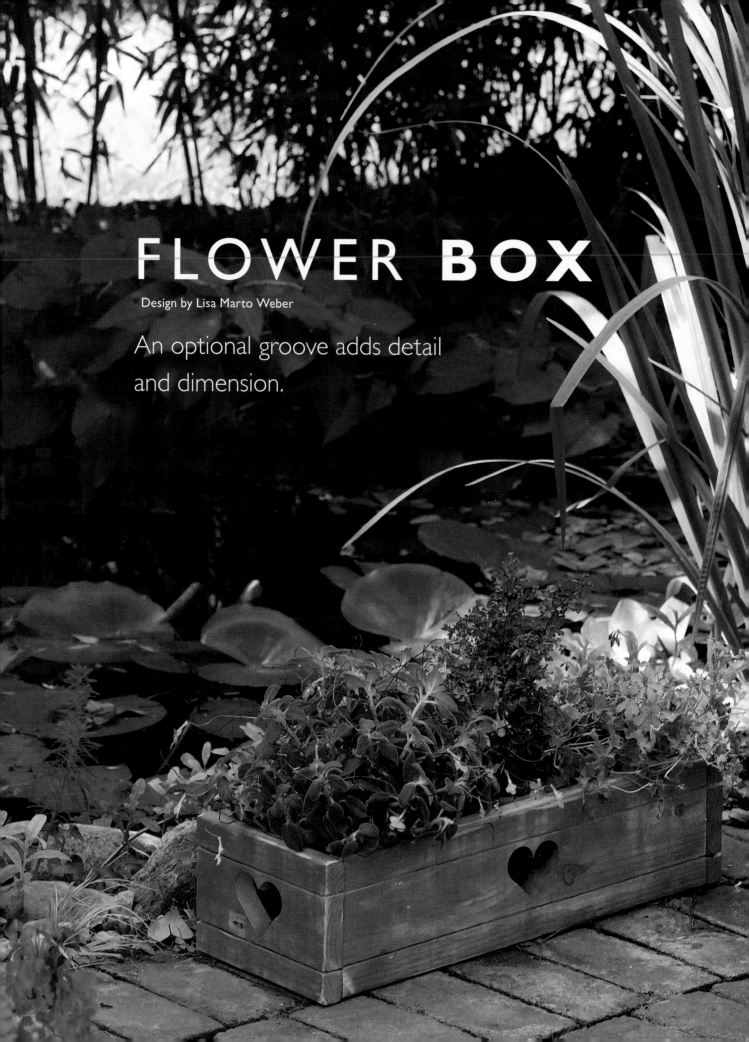

FLOWER BOX

Design by Lisa Marto Weber

An optional groove adds detail
and dimension.

CUTTING

1 Measure and cut 1x6 cedar lumber into three 20-inch lengths (A) and two 7½-inch lengths (B).

2 Set aside two 20-inch lengths (A) for back and bottom. Make a groove in each of three remaining wood pieces (one A and two B) for front and ends as follows: Raise table saw blade to ⅛ inch above table. Measure 1½ inches down from top and up from bottom of each board; run boards through table saw, cutting grooves.

3 Using graphite paper, transfer heart pattern onto center of each front and end board. Drill a ½-inch hole in center of each heart; beginning in each hole, cut out hearts with jigsaw.

ASSEMBLE & FINISH

1 Place one 20-inch 1x6 (A) onto flat work surface for bottom of box. Attach remaining 20-inch 1x6s (A) to each edge of bottom for front and back with glue and nails. Attach 7½-inch 1x6s (B) to front, back and bottom for ends. Fill nail holes with wood putty and sand, following manufacturer's directions.

2 Sand flower box and remove dust with tack cloth. Finish as desired with exterior paint or stain. Let dry, then sand lightly to give an aged appearance. ✸

Flower Box Heart

FLOWER BOX CUTTING CHART

P	T	W	L	#
A	1"	6"	20"	3
B	1"	6"	7½"	2

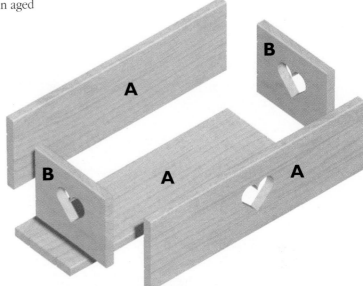

PROJECT SIZE
22x7½x5½ inches

TOOLS
• Jigsaw
• Table saw (for optional grooves in wood)
• Drill with ½-inch bit
• Nail gun with 1½-inch nails or 1½-inch finish nails and hammer

SUPPLIES
• 1x6 stock cedar: 7 feet
• Graphite paper
• Exterior wood glue
• Wood putty
• Putty knife
• Medium-grit sandpaper
• Tack cloth
• Exterior paint or stain

REFLECTIONS PLANTER

Design by Barbara Matthiessen

This trendy, mirrored planter will look lovely on a deck or patio. For a final touch, attach it to a wall or privacy fence with brass screws.

PROJECT NOTE

To extend the life of the planter, coat inside with exterior varnish, or line with plastic or roofing paper before filling.

CUTTING

1 Cut 70-inch 1x4 into one 14³⁄₈-inch length (A) and one 15-inch length (B) for sides, and one each 22-inch length (C), 13-inch length (E) and 6-inch length (F) for front pieces.

2 Cut 32-inch ¼x¾-inch screen molding into two 15¾-inch lengths (G) for trim. Using a miter box, cut a 45-degree angle on one end of each piece.

ASSEMBLE & FINISH

1 Referring to diagram, position 1x4 sides (A and B) on plywood base. Using ¹⁄₁₆-inch bit, predrill every 3 inches through plywood back into 1x4 sides; attach sides to base with galvanized screws.

2 Beginning at bottom point of frame with shortest piece, position remaining 1x4s (C, E and

F) and 1x2 (D) across front of frame; mark sides of frame on underside of each piece to establish cutting lines, then cut each piece to correct length. Attach front pieces to sides with wood glue and finish nails.

3 Using wood glue and finish nails, attach 15¾-inch trim (G) to top edge of planter. Drill a ⅛-inch hole in top peak of planter under attached screen molding, for hanging.

4 Fill visible screw and nail holes with wood putty and sand following manufacturer's directions.

5 Apply one coat of paint to assembled piece; let dry. Sand edges lightly for an aged appearance.

6 Following manufacturer's directions, use mirror/glass cutter and straight edge to cut mirror tile in half diagonally. Attach

mirror tile to planter by applying a generous amount of mirror adhesive tape to back of mirror and pressing firmly in place. Allow adhesive to cure according to manufacturer's directions.

7 Attach planter to fence or wall by inserting 1½-inch brass screw in hole at top peak. ✿

PROJECT SIZE
15¾x15⅞x4⅜ inches

TOOLS
- Handsaw
- Miter box
- Straight edge
- Drill with 1/16-inch and ⅛-inch bits
- Hammer
- Phillips head screwdriver

SUPPLIES
- 15¾x15¾x⅜-inch AC plywood
- 1x4: 6 feet pine or cedar
- 1x2: 2 feet pine or cedar
- ¼x¾-inch screen molding: 3 feet length
- One 12-inch-square mirror tile
- Eleven 1-inch No. 6 Phillips head galvanized screws
- Exterior wood glue
- 1¼-inch finish nails
- Wood putty
- Sandpaper
- White acrylic exterior house paint
- Paintbrush
- Mirror/glass cutter
- Mirror adhesive tape
- One 1½-inch No. 10 brass screw

REFLECTIONS PLANTER CUTTING CHART

P	T	W	L	#
A	1"	4"	14⅜"	1
B	1"	4"	15"	1
C	1"	4"	22"	1
D	1"	2"	16"	1
E	1"	4"	13"	1
F	1"	4"	6"	1
G	¼"	¾"	15¾"	2

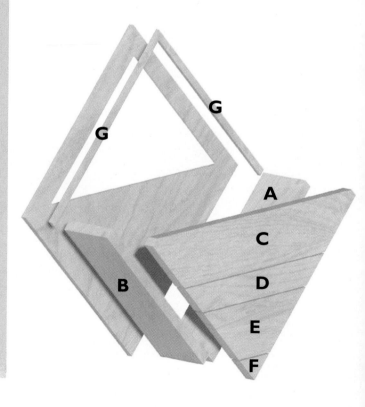

SAIL AWAY NAPKIN HOLDERS

Design by Mary Nelson

Invite your friends over for a casual barbecue and use these cheerful napkin holders. Both the lighthouse and the sailboat motifs can be cut with your scroll saw.

PROJECT NOTES

When shading, highlighting, lining and spattering, thin paints with water to an ink consistency.

Allow paints to dry after each coat, and before applying adjacent colors.

CUTTING

1 Using graphite paper, transfer outline of sails, flag and boat (for sailboat) and lighthouse onto ¹⁄₁₆-inch Baltic birch; cut out using scroll saw; sand edges smooth with detail sander or sandpaper.

2 For each napkin holder top, cut ½-inch-thick pine board 5⅞x6⅜-inches. Drill ⅜-inch holes as indicated on pattern. Sand edges smooth with belt sander or sandpaper.

3 Cut ¼-inch poplar into two 7x½-inch strips and two 6⅜x½-inch strips. Cut a 45-degree angle on one end of each strip. Dry-fit pieces around pine board piece, continuing to cut small pieces to achieve a good fit. Sand rough edges.

4 For each napkin holder base, cut a 7½x7½-inch square from ¼-inch-thick plywood. Position napkin holder top on base, centered between sides with top edges even. Mark hole placement on base; drill with ⁵⁄₁₆-inch bit.

5 Cut ⁵⁄₁₆-inch dowel into two 3½-inch lengths.

ASSEMBLE & FINISH

1 Glue and clamp poplar strips around top. Fill gaps with wood putty and sand, following manufacturer's directions. Let dry.

2 Fit dowels into holes in base; glue into place. Fit top onto base over dowels, adjusting as needed so top slides freely. Let glue dry thoroughly.

3 With buttermilk, base-coat entire surfaces of top and base, including dowels, applying multiple coats as needed to cover.

4 With sable brown, stencil checkerboard pattern across top edge of top and side and bottom edges of base. Outline checks with burnt umber.

5 For sailboat napkin holder, use graphite paper to transfer outlines for sailboat onto top. Mask off areas for sails, boat and banner with masking tape. Paint background below checkerboard

pattern with soft blue. Lightly transfer outline for sun onto top. Using photo and pattern as guides, paint top and birch sailboat pieces as follows:

Waves—deep periwinkle; highlight tops of waves with white wash. **Sun**—yellow ochre; shade with true ochre. Blush cheeks with antique mauve. With lamp black, dot the

PROJECT SIZE
7½x7½x3½ inches

TOOLS
- Scroll saw
- Detail sander (optional)
- Table saw
- Belt sander (optional)
- Drill with 5/16-inch and 3/8-inch bits
- Quick grip clamps

SUPPLIES
- 1/16-inch-thick Baltic birch
- ¼-inch-thick plywood
- ½-inch-thick pine
- ¼-inch-thick poplar
- 5/16-inch dowel
- Graphite paper
- Sandpaper
- Wood glue
- Wood putty
- Masking tape
- Americana acrylic paints from DecoArt:
  (for both projects) buttermilk #DA3, sable brown #DA61, burnt umber #DA64, whitewash #DA2, midnight blue #DA85, Napa red #DA165, true ochre #DA143, lamp black #DA67; (for sailboat) soft blue #DA210, deep periwinkle #DA212, yellow ochre #DA8, antique mauve #DA162; (for lighthouse) baby blue #DA42, forest green #DA50, Hauser medium green #DA132, Hauser dark green #DA133
- Paintbrushes
- Toothpicks
- ¼-inch check stencil
- ½-inch stencil brush
- Acrylic spray sealer

eyes and line mouth and eyebrows. Use toothpick and white wash to make tiny dots for highlights on cheeks and eyes.

Sail pole—lamp black.

Right sail—white wash with deep periwinkle blue stripes; outline with lamp black.

Bottom portion of left sail—

\whitewash with Napa red stripes; outline with lamp black.

Top portion of left sail—midnight blue with true ochre stars; outline with lamp black.

Banner—Napa red with true ochre stripes.

Boat—Napa red; line boat name with whitewash.

6 For lighthouse napkin holder, use graphite paper to transfer outlines for lighthouse and shore line onto top. Mask off area for lighthouse with masking tape. Paint background below checkerboard pattern, using baby blue for water and forest green for shore. Lightly transfer outline for sailboat onto top. Using photo and pattern as guides, paint top and birch

lighthouse pieces as follows:

Waves—midnight blue; highlight with whitewash.

Trees—pounce Hauser medium green over forest green; shade with Hauser dark green

Sailboat—whitewash; paint pole lamp black; paint banner and stripes on left sail midnight blue; paint star on right sail true ochre.

Lighthouse—base-coat with buttermilk; paint roofs and line windows and parapet with lamp black; paint stripes with Napa red; shade with sable brown.

7 Remove masking tape. Glue sailboat and lighthouse onto tops, clamping until dry.

8 Spatter the tops with whitewash, followed by burnt umber, then lamp black.

9 Spray all pieces with two coats of acrylic sealer, following manufacturer's directions. ❋

SERVING TRAY

Design by Cindy Reusser

Let the summer float by in a gentle breeze as you enjoy your nautical serving tray with rope handles. Using a miter box makes the cutting easier.

INSTRUCTIONS

1 Set miter box to make a 45-degree angle cut; cut 24-inch 1x2s into two 20-inch lengths and two 13½-inch lengths (outside dimensions).

2 Referring to photo for placement, assemble cut pieces to form tray sides, using wood glue and 1½-inch nails.

3 Attach ¼-inch Luan to bottom of tray sides using glue and ¾-inch brads. Fill nail holes with wood putty and sand following manufacturer's directions.

PROJECT SIZE
20x13½x2¼ inches

TOOLS
• Miter box
• Drill with ⅜-inch bit
• Nail gun with 1½-inch nails, or 1½-inch finish nails
• Corner clamps (optional)

SUPPLIES
• 1x2: four 24-inch lengths
• 20x13½x¼-inch Luan or paneling
• Wood glue
• 1½-inch nails
• ¾-inch brads
• Wood putty
• Sandpaper
• 2-inch foam brush
• Acrylic paint: red, ivory, black, brown, blue
• Graphite paper
• Paintbrushes
• Spray sealer
• 36 inches ⅜-inch sisal rope

4 Drill two ⅜-inch holes 4 inches apart in center of each 13½ side.

5 Using foam brush, paint tray with ivory; let dry.

6 Transfer sailboat pattern onto tray with graphite paper. Paint as follows:

Boat—Paint with red; shade interior brown; outline and add detail with black.

Flag—Paint with blue; outline with black.

Sail—Shade with brown; outline with black.

Pole—Paint with black.

Waves—Add with blue.

7 Let dry. Spray tray with acrylic sealer; let dry.

8 Cut rope into two 18-inch lengths. On each end of tray, insert ends of rope from outside to inside through ⅜-inch holes; knot ends on inside and trim ends to form handles. ❉

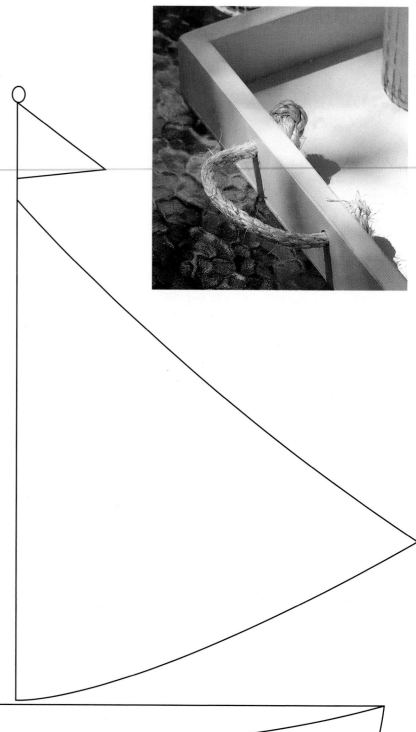

**Serving Tray
Sailboat**

TRIVET TRIO

Design by Bev Shenefield

Make a great set of trivets for your next barbecue. Be sure to place the trivets in a well-ventilated area on a heat-resistant surface when trying this popular technique for finishing with a propane torch.

PROJECT NOTES

Follow manufacturer's instructions for using propane torch.

Work in a well-ventilated area on a heat-resistant surface when using torch.

Use propane torch on low to medium flame, holding 3 to 6 inches from project surface and moving in a back-and-forth motion until desired depth of color is achieved.

CUTTING

1 Use handsaw to cut wood strips as follows:

Square trivet—Cut five 6-inch pieces; sand ends.

Round trivet—Cut two 9-inch, two 8-inch and two 7-inch pieces.

Triangle trivet—Enlarge pattern 135 percent. Use enlarged pattern to mark and cut angles for each piece; sand ends.

2 Hold each piece in vise and drill a ¼-inch hole in center of 1½-inch side.

ASSEMBLE & FINISH

1 For square and triangle trivets only, burn sides and ends of each wood strip; apply varnish to sides only. Let dry. For round trivet, burn sides only of each piece. **Note:** *Ends will be cut, sanded and burned, and sides will be varnished after assembly.*

2 Use hacksaw to cut threaded rod into 6¾-inch, 8¼-inch and 9½-inch lengths; file cut ends.

PROJECT SIZE
Square trivet: 6x7x1½ inches
Round trivet: 7¾x8½x1½ inches
Triangle trivet: 10¼x9¾x1½ inches

TOOLS
• Handsaw
• Hacksaw
• Jigsaw
• Vise
• Propane torch
• Drill with ¼-inch bit
• Needle-nose pliers
• Metal file

SUPPLIES
• 1x2 cabinet pine: four 48-inch lengths
• Sandpaper
• Clear satin varnish
• Paintbrush
• Thirty-six inches ¼-inch threaded rod
• Six ¼-inch acorn nuts
• The Ultimate glue by Crafter's Pick
• Forty-five ¼-inch hex nuts
• Eleven ½-inch vinyl pads

3 For square trivet, place acorn nut on one end of 6¾-inch rod; insert rod into one wood strip then add three nuts, tightening each one as tight as possible with pliers before adding the next. Continue adding wood strips alternately with nuts. Add acorn nut to top.

4 For round trivet, place acorn nut on one end of 8¼-inch rod; insert rod into one 7-inch wood strip then add three nuts as for square trivet. Continue adding wood strips alternately with nuts as follows: 8-inch, two 9-inch, 8-inch and 7-inch. Add acorn nut to top. Enlarge pattern 135 percent. Use enlarged pattern to draw circle in center of assembled wood pieces; cut with jigsaw. Sand ends and burn. Apply varnish to sides; let dry.

5 For triangle trivet, place acorn nut on one end of 9½-inch rod; insert rod into largest wood strip then add three nuts as for square trivet. Continue adding wood strips alternately with nuts, from largest to smallest piece. Add acorn nut to top. **Note:** *To assure sufficient tightening, add glue to hole in each wood strip before inserting rod.*

6 Apply vinyl pads to bottoms of each trivet. ✿

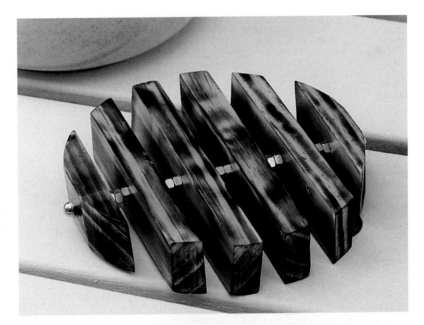

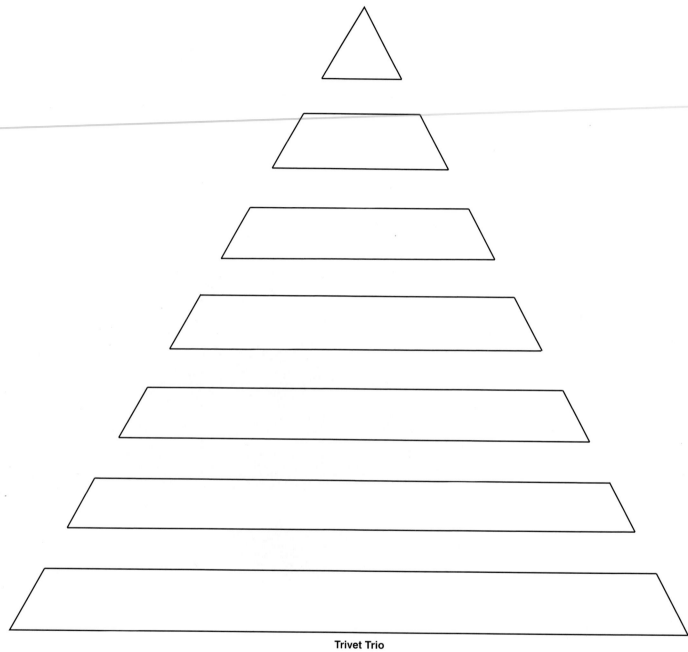

Trivet Trio
Triangle Trivet
Enlarge pattern 135%

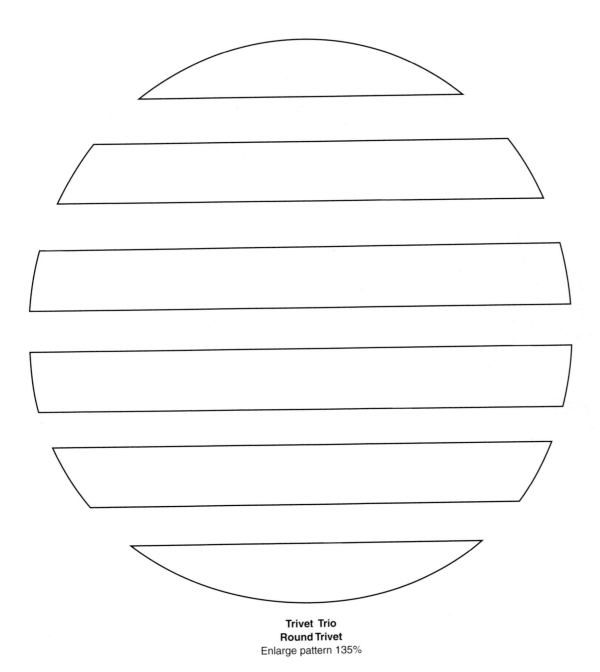

Trivet Trio
Round Trivet
Enlarge pattern 135%

BARBECUE CADDY

Design by Bev Shenefield

An easy-to-achieve finish provides a unique wood grain look.

PROJECT NOTES

Follow manufacturer's instructions for using propane torch.

Work in a well-ventilated area on a heat-resistant surface when using torch.

Keep the propane torch 3 to 6 inches from project surface moving in a back and forth motion until the desired depth of color is achieved.

Burn all project pieces before assembly.

INSTRUCTIONS

1 Apply wood glue to wrong side of one paddle plaque 6 inches from bottom of the plaque; center against end of wooden box with bottom edges even. Attach with nails through inside of box. Repeat with remaining plaque on opposite end of box.

2 Position dowel handle between tops of paddle plaques; mark through holes in top of plaques onto dowel. Drill a ³⁄₁₆-inch pilot hole in each end of dowel; attach dowel with 1¼-inch deck screws.

3 Glue 5¾x3x¼-inch pieces (A) pine 2 inches apart onto the 7x5¾x¾-inch pine board (B) to create divider; let dry. Apply varnish to all surfaces except bottom and outside edges; let dry. Glue divider inside bottom left end of box.

4 Apply varnish to remainder of box; let dry ✹

P	T	W	L	#
BARBECUE CADDY CUTTING CHART				
A	3"	¼"	5¾"	3
B	7"	¾"	5¾"	1

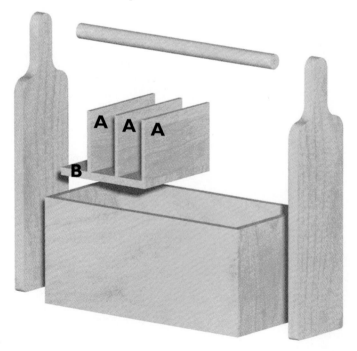

PROJECT SIZE
16x6½x19 inches

TOOLS
- Drill with ³⁄₁₆-inch bit
- Phillips head screwdriver
- Propane torch

SUPPLIES
- Three 5¾x3x¼-inch pieces pine
- 7x5¾x¾-inch pine board
- 14½x6½x6½-inch wooden box
- Two 5x18-inch paddle plaques
- Sand-N-Stain Wood Glue from
  Crafter's Pick
- Twelve ¾-inch nails
- 14³⁄₈ inches 1-inch wooden dowel
- Two 1¼-inch deck screws
- Clear gloss varnish

HONEYBEES FEEDER

Design by Mary Nelson

Treat your guests to a snack as they kick back and relax.

CUTTING

1 Using patterns provided, cut two sides (A) and one base (B) from ¾-inch pine; cut back (C), roof back (E), roof front (F) and roof plug (G) from ½-inch pine; cut roof plug top (H) from Baltic birch plywood. Cut ¼-inch poplar into three 1x6-inch strips (D). Sand edges and wipe with tack cloth.

2 Use table saw to cut a ⅛-inch-wide and ¼-inch deep groove on each side where indicated on pattern (saw kerf).

3 Use pattern provided to cut acrylic (I) with scroll saw. **Note:** *Leave protective plastic on acrylic until you are ready to slide it into grooves of painted feeder.*

ASSEMBLE & FINISH

1 Apply wood glue to bottom edges of sides (A); place on base (B); insert No. 8 wood screws through bottom of base into sides to secure. Use glue and finish nails to nail back (C) between side pieces.

2 Glue a 1x6-inch strip (D) across bottom front of feeder; glue remaining 1x6-inch strips (D) to bottom sides of feeder; secure with wire brads.

3 Referring to pattern for placement, cut a 2-inch-diameter hole in roof back (E). Position roof back (E) and roof front (F) together with front overlapping back to form a 90-degree angle. Apply glue and nail with finish nails. Glue roof plug (G) in center of roof plug top (H); clamp until dry

4 Use nail set to set all nails and brads. Fill and sand holes with wood putty following manufacturer's

directions. Sand project and wipe with tack cloth.

5 Use masking tape to mask off all interior portions of bird feeder. Base-coat sides and back with Hauser dark green; base-coat roof, roof plug/top and bottom strips with golden straw. Let dry. Stencil asphaltum checks around outside of bottom strips.

6 Transfer design to roof front; paint as follows:
Note: Allow drying time between colors.
Branches—line with asphaltum.
Leaves—Hauser dark green.
Beehive—honey brown; shade and line with asphaltum.
Beehive opening—lamp black.
Honeybees—using tip of

paintbrush handle, dot bodies with true ochre; dot heads with lamp black. Paint wings and stripes with lamp black.

7 Thin buttermilk, asphaltum and lamp black with water to an ink consistency; use old toothbrush to spatter each color over birdhouse; let dry.

PROJECT SIZE
6½x7x9½ inches

TOOLS
• Table saw
• Scroll saw with #5 blade
• Clamp
• Nail set

SUPPLIES
• 24x6x¾-inch pine
• 18x6x½-inch pine
• 3x6x¼-inch poplar or pine
• Scrap of ⅛-inch Baltic birch plywood at least 3½ inches square
• Sandpaper
• Tack cloth
• 4¼x6x⅛-inch clear acrylic
• Wood glue
• 1¾-inch No. 8 wood screws
• 1¼-inch finish nails
• ¾-inch No. 18 wire brads
• Wood putty
• Masking tape
• Americana acrylic paint from DecoArt: buttermilk #DA03, lamp black #DA67, Hauser dark green #DA133, true ochre #DA143, honey brown #DA163, golden straw #DA168 and asphaltum #DA180
• ¼-inch check stencil
• Paintbrushes
• Old toothbrush
• Matte spray sealer

8 Spray birdhouse with two coats of sealer, letting dry after each coat. Remove masking tape.

9 Remove protective plastic from acrylic (I); insert into grooves on sides. Screw roof back to sides with wood screws. ✿

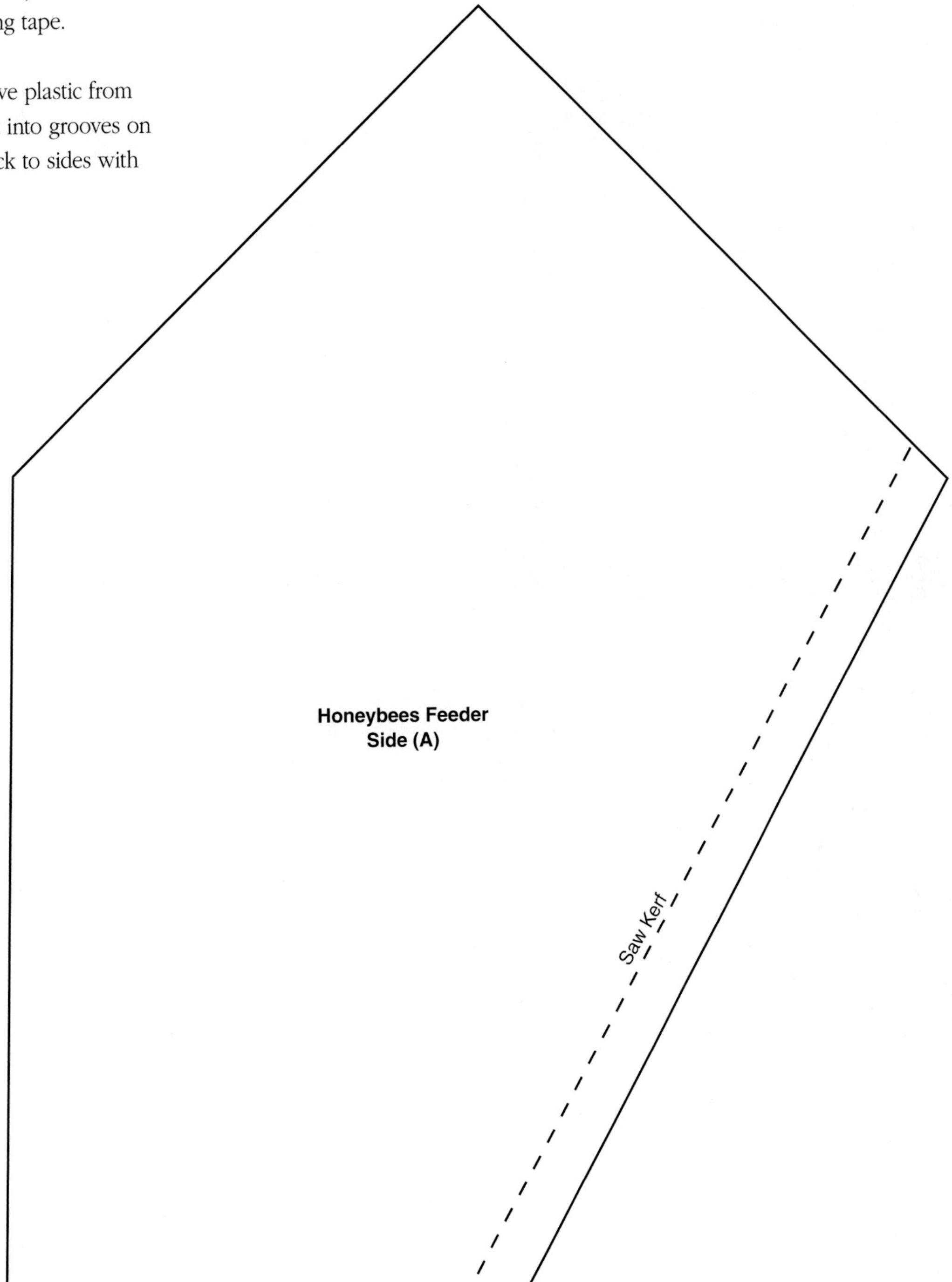

**Honeybees Feeder
Side (A)**

Saw Kerf

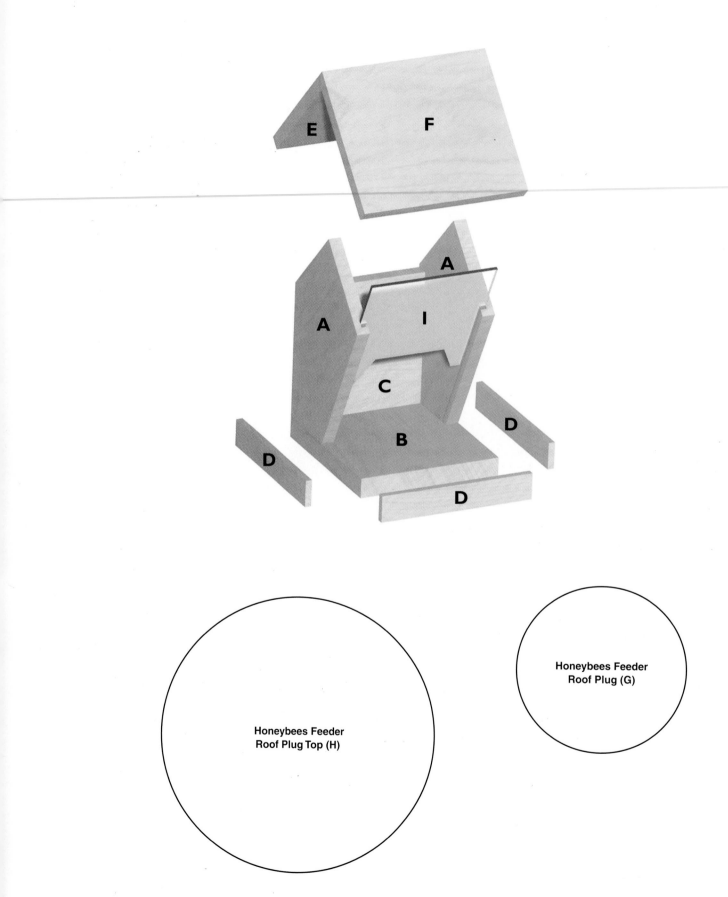

Honeybees Feeder
Roof Plug Top (H)

Honeybees Feeder
Roof Plug (G)

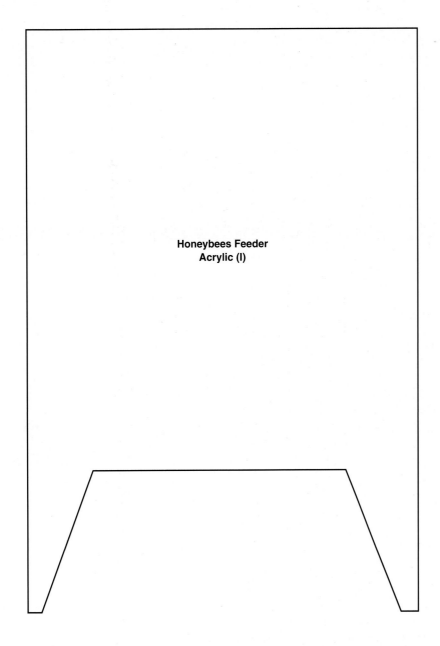

Honeybees Feeder
Acrylic (l)

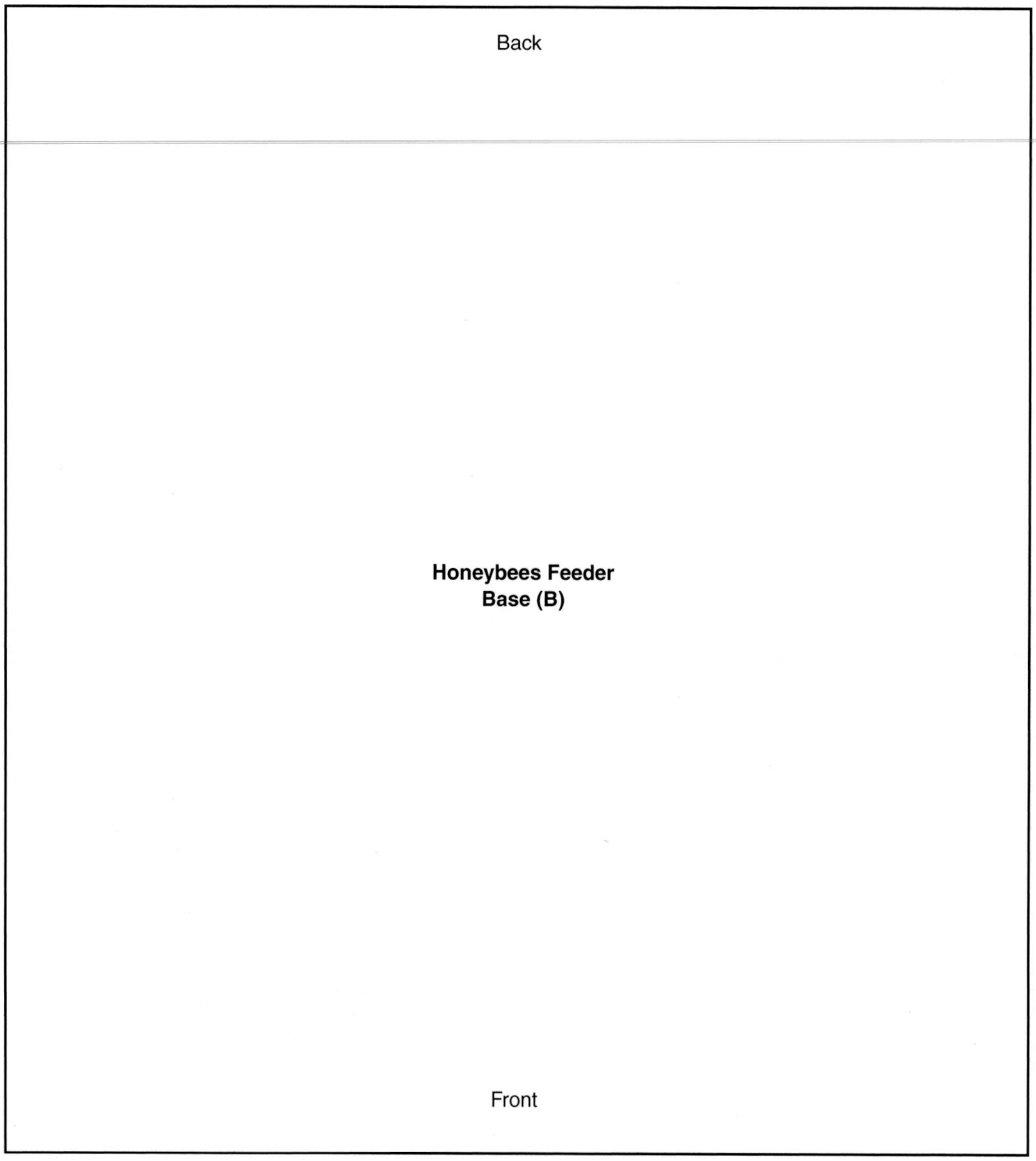

Back

Honeybees Feeder
Base (B)

Front

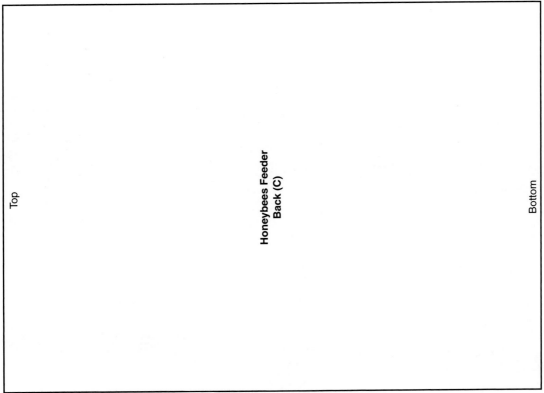

Top

**Honeybees Feeder
Back (C)**

Bottom

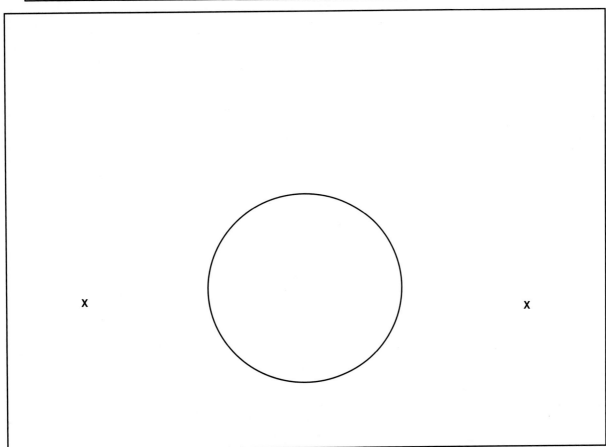

X   X

**Honeybees Feeder
Roof Back (E)**

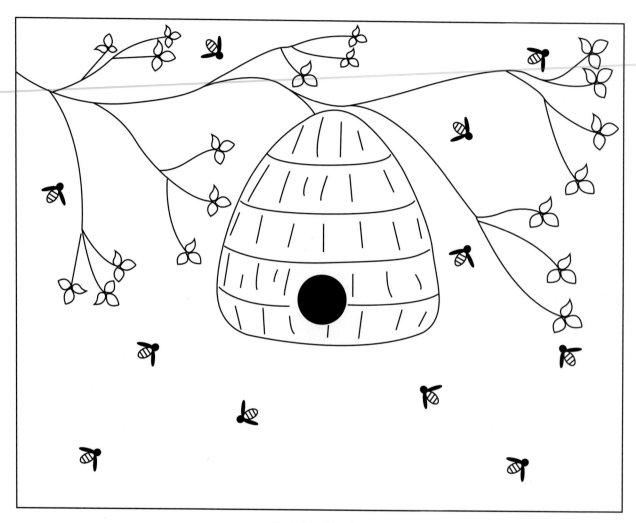

**Honeybees Feeder
Roof Front (F)**

FLOWER PRESS

Design by Mary Ayres

Have fun pressing the flowers that you have grown
with your own loving care.

PROJECT NOTES

To stencil design, dip a dry stencil brush in paint. Wipe brush on a paper towel, removing excess paint to prevent seepage under stencil. Brush cut out areas with a circular motion, holding brush perpendicular to the surface.

When shading, brush should be almost dry, working only around the edges.

DRILLING

1 Place two 5½x6½-inch wood rectangles on top of each other with scrap block of wood underneath. With edges even, drill a ¼-inch hole ½-inch from each corner through both pieces of wood. Sand both pieces until smooth.

GOLD BORDER

1 Using a metal ruler and craft knife, cut masking tape into ½-inch- and ¼-inch-wide strips. Place ½-inch-wide strips around all four sides of one wood rectangle with edges of tape even with edges of wood rectangle. Use ¼-inch-wide strips to mask off area for gold border (Photo 1).

2 Paint the ¼-inch border between taped areas with glorious gold (Photo 2). Remove tape when finished (Photo 3).

STENCILING

1 Position flower stencil on wood piece, centered inside gold border. Following manufacturer's directions, stencil as follows:

Daisy center—golden straw; shade with honey brown; stencil dots with jade green.

Daisy petals—cool white; shade with slate grey.

Large purple flowers—orchid; shade with lavender.

Medium blue flowers—baby blue; shade with sapphire; stencil centers with royal fuchsia and dots in centers with sapphire.

Tiny heart-shaped flowers—baby pink; shade with royal fuchsia.

Dots above fern-shaped leaf—golden straw.

Remaining dots—stencil with darker shade of corresponding flower color.

Leaves—jade green; shade with leaf green.

Stems—leaf green.

ASSEMBLE

1 On each cardboard and paper rectangle, mark 1¼ inches from each corner on each edge. Draw a line across each corner using marks as a guide; cut on diagonal lines.

2 Place two papers between each cardboard rectangle. Stack cardboard rectangles together and place between wood rectangles with stenciled design on top.

3 Place washers on bolts and insert bolts from bottom through holes in wood rectangles. Attach wing nuts tightly onto bolts.

PRESSING

1 Remove top from press. Gather flowers or leaves for pressing in the morning after dew has dried; immediately place between papers and cardboard in press.

2 Replace wood top and screw wing nuts tightly onto bolts.

3 Leave flowers in press several weeks to dry. ✿

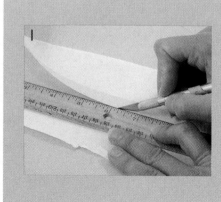

PROJECT SIZE
5½x6½ inches

TOOLS
• Drill with ¼-inch bit

SUPPLIES
• Two 5½x6½x¼-inch pieces wood
• Scrap block of wood
• Fine-grit sandpaper
• Metal ruler
• Craft knife
• Paintbrushes: ¼-inch stencil and #5 round
• Americana acrylic paint from DecoArt: jade green #DA57, leaf green #DA51, baby blue #DA42, sapphire #DA99, golden straw #DA168, orchid #DA33, honey brown #DA163, baby pink #DA31, royal fuchsia #DA151, cool white #DA240, slate grey #DA68, lavender #DA34
• Dazzling Metallics acrylic metallic paint from DecoArt: glorious gold #DA71
• Wildflower Bouquet #CS-33 4x5-inch Classic Dimensions Sentiments overlay stencil from American Traditional Designs
• Seven 5¼x6¼-inch rectangles of ⅛-inch-thick corrugated cardboard.
• Twelve 5⅛x6¼-inch sheets white paper (computer printer paper works well)
• Four ¼-inch brass washers
• Four ¼x2-inch brass bolts
• Four ¼-inch brass wing nuts
• Pencil
• Paper towels
• Masking tape

SHABBY-CHIC-STYLE SCROLL THERMOMETER

Design by Barbara Greve

Hang this on your deck or patio and you will always know what the temperature is. Some of the materials can be bought premade, but if you are adventurous, you can always cut them out with your scroll saw.

PROJECT SIZE
12x8 x1½ inches

TOOLS
• Scroll saw with #5 blade

SUPPLIES
• 12x8x1½-inch wooden scroll bracket
• Fine-grit sandpaper
• Paper towels
• 2¾-inch-diameter ivory dial thermometer insert #32126 from Klockit
• Pencil
• All-purpose sealer
• Acrylic paint: burnt umber, brown and white
• Paintbrushes
• Paint palette
• Brown antiquing gel
• Matte varnish
• Silicone glue

CUTTING

1 Sand any rough spots smooth on scroll bracket; remove dust with damp paper towel.

2 Postion thermometer insert over scroll portion of bracket. Referring to Fig. 1, use pencil to mark back of thermometer onto scroll; cut away portion of scroll with scroll saw to accommodate insert. Sand smooth and remove dust with damp paper towel.

3 Seal bracket with all-purpose sealer; let dry. Sand smooth and remove dust with damp paper towel.

PAINTING

1 Mix two parts burnt umber with one part brown; base-coat bracket. Let dry two hours.

**Shabby-Chic-Style Scroll Thermometer
Fig. 1**
Cut off a portion of scroll (shaded area) to accommodate insert.

2 Paint over base coat with white; set aside until dry to the touch. Sand lightly, exposing base coat to achieve distressed look.

3 Seal brass rim of thermometer with all-purpose sealer; let dry. Apply brown antiquing gel to sealed rim and wipe off to achieve desired look.

4 Apply two coats of matte varnish to bracket, letting dry after each coat.

ASSEMBLE & FINISH

1 Glue insert in bracket; let dry. ✸

Yards

TULIP DECORATIVE FENCE

Design by Rue Ann Flanders

If you enjoy using your scroll saw, you will love creating this fence with its beautiful floral design. Can't you just see a row of tulips waving in the breeze in front of this portable fence? Because the fence stands on its own, you can easily move it the next time you mow.

PROJECT NOTES

If router is not available, notching for fence rail placement can be done with a hammer and wood chisel, or check at your local lumberyard about custom cutting.

When drilling holes for decorative design, use a backing board to minimize tearout.

CUTTING

1 For fence boards, draw a line across each 36-inch 1x6, 3⅛ inches from top; mark center of line. Insert point of compass at this point to draw rounded edge tops of fence boards. Cut with jigsaw or scroll saw.

2 Enlarge decorative pattern 200 percent. Tape pattern on fence board, positioning top of design 11¼ inches from top of board. Transfer design to board with graphite paper. Repeat for three more boards.

3 Beginning with top and bottom designs, drill out circles using ¹⁵⁄₆₄-inch bit. Next, use a ¼-inch bit to drill two holes next to each other for heart; cut out remainder of heart with a jigsaw or scroll saw. Cut circular part of tulips with ⅞-inch drill bit; finish cutting tulips with jigsaw or scroll saw.

4 Drill circles in middle tulip design, using ⅜-inch bit to drill largest circles, ¹⁵⁄₆₄-inch bit to drill next-size circles and ⅛-inch bit to drill smallest circles. Cut and drill heart as for top and bottom designs, using ⁵⁄₁₆-inch bit. Drill and cut tulips as for top and bottom designs, using 1⅛-inch bit.

5 Sand edges of design cutouts smooth.

ASSEMBLE & FINISH

1 On a flat surface, lay out two 37¼-inch 4x4s for fence posts. On each post, draw a line 5 inches from top; draw another line 3½ inches below top line. Draw a line 4½ inches from bottom; draw another line 3½ inches above bottom line. Using band saw, make a 1½-inch-deep cut on each line; cut away area between each pair of lines using router or other method.

2 Position 68-inch 2x4s between fence posts for top and bottom rails, fitting 2x4s into cutout sections on posts with ends flush. Secure rails to posts with four 2½-inch wood screws in each end.

3 For feet, bevel top edge on each end of each 12-inch 2x4. Temporarily clamp one foot into place on bottom of post,

centered lengthwise and running perpendicular to fence rails. Using 1-inch forstner bit, drill two holes on the bottom of the foot deep enough to sink the head of a lag screw; with $\frac{9}{32}$-inch bit, drill through centers of 1-inch holes into post. Slip washers onto lag bolts; drive lag bolts into holes using a ratchet and $\frac{1}{2}$-inch socket. Repeat for remaining foot.

4 Using photo as a guide, lay out fence boards along fence rails having bottoms flush with bottoms of posts and spacing $1\frac{7}{8}$ inches apart.

5 For each fence board, temporarily clamp board into place; drill and countersink two holes at each point where fence board and fence rails meet. Secure board with 2-inch wood screws.

6 Attach fence-post caps to tops of posts with exterior wood glue.

7 Prime fence with exterior primer and paint following manufacturer's directions. Finish with clear exterior polyurethane for added durability. ❁

PROJECT SIZE
75x39½ inches

TOOLS
- Compass
- Jigsaw or scroll saw
- Band saw
- Router (optional)
- Drill with ⅜-inch, ⁵⁄₁₆-inch, ⁹⁄₃₂-inch, ¼-inch, ¹⁵⁄₆₄-inch and ⅛-inch brad point bits, 1⅛-inch, 1-inch and ⅞-inch forstner or paddle bits, and countersink attachment
- Clamps
- Ratchet with ½-inch socket

SUPPLIES
- 1x6 poplar: nine 36-inch lengths
- 2x4 cedar or redwood: two 68-inch lengths and two 12-inch lengths
- 4x4 cedar or redwood: two 37¼-inch lengths
- Two fence-post caps
- Graphite paper
- Sandpaper
- Framing square
- Backing board
- Exterior wood screws: sixteen 2½-inch and thirty-six 2-inch
- Four 5¹⁄₁₆x3½-inch lag screws with washers
- Exterior wood glue
- Exterior primer and paint
- Clear exterior polyurethane (optional)

Tulip Decorative Fence
Enlarge pattern 200%

BERRY BRANCH DECORATIVE FENCE

Design by Rue Ann Flanders

Create a "berry" beautiful and portable fence section for your yard. It makes a great backdrop for a small flowerbed. It's also a good way to divide the play and garden areas of your yard.

PROJECT NOTE

If router is not available, notching for fence rail placement can be done with a hammer and wood chisel, or check at your local lumberyard about custom cutting.

CUTTING

1 For fence boards, draw a line across each 36-inch 1x6, 3⅛ inches from top; mark center of line. Insert point of compass at this point to draw rounded edge tops of fence boards. Cut with jigsaw or scroll saw.

2 Enlarge decorative pattern 200 percent. Tape pattern on fence board, positioning top of design 11¼ inches from top of board. Transfer design to board with graphite paper. Repeat for three more boards.

3 Drill out the holes for berries with ⅜-inch brad point bit. **Note:** *Use a backing board underneath fence board to minimize tearout on the backside.*

4 Cut out remainder of design with jigsaw or scroll saw. Sand edges of design cutouts smooth.

ASSEMBLE & FINISH

1 On a flat surface, lay out two 37¼-inch 4x4s for fence posts. On each post, draw a line 5 inches from top; draw another line 3½ inches below top line. Draw a line 4½ inches from bottom; draw another line 3½ inches above bottom line. Using band saw, make a 1½-inch-deep cut on each line; cut away area between each pair of lines using router or other method.

2 Position 68-inch 2x4s between fence posts for top and bottom rails, fitting 2x4s into cutout sections on posts with ends flush. Secure rails to posts with four 2½-inch wood screws in each end.

3 For feet, bevel top edge on each end of each 12-inch 2x4. Temporarily clamp one foot into place on bottom of post, centered lengthwise and running perpendicular to fence rails. Using 1-inch forstner bit, drill two holes on the bottom of the foot deep enough to sink the head of a lag screw; with ⁹⁄₃₂-inch bit, drill through centers of 1-inch holes into post. Slip washers onto lag bolts; drive lag bolts into holes using a ratchet and ½-inch socket. Repeat for remaining foot.

4 Using photo as a guide, lay out fence boards along fence rails having bottoms flush with bottoms of posts and spacing 1⅞ inches apart.

5 For each fence board, temporarily clamp board into place; drill and countersink two holes at each point where fence board and fence rails meet. Secure board with 2-inch wood screws.

6 Attach fence-post caps to tops of posts with exterior wood glue.

7 If desired, prime fence with exterior primer and paint, following manufacturer's directions. Finish with clear exterior polyurethane for added durability. ❁

PROJECT SIZE
75x39½ inches

TOOLS
• Compass
• Jigsaw or scroll saw
• Band saw
• Router (optional)
• Drill with ⁹⁄₃₂-inch and ⅜-inch brad point
    bits, 1-inch forstner or paddle bit, and
    countersink attachment
• Clamps
• Ratchet with ½-inch socket

SUPPLIES
• 1x6 poplar: nine 36-inch lengths
• 2x4 cedar or western pine: two 68-inch
    lengths and two 12-inch lengths
• 4x4 cedar or western pine: two 37¼-inch
    lengths
• Two fence-post caps
• Graphite paper
• Sandpaper
• Framing square
• Backing board
• Exterior wood screws: sixteen 2½-inch and
    thirty-six 2-inch
• Four 5¹⁄₁₆x3½-inch lag screws with washers
• Exterior wood glue
• Exterior primer and paint
• Clear exterior polyurethane (optional)

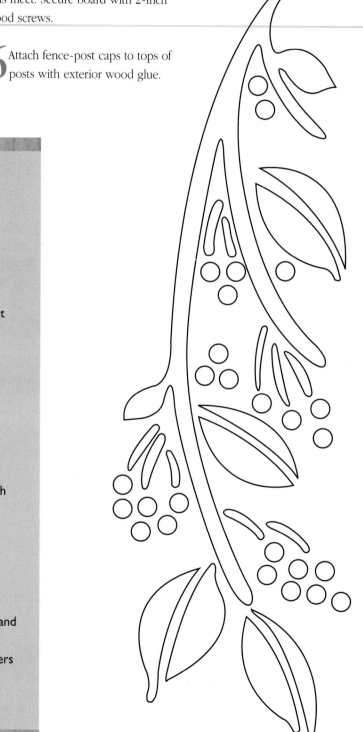

Berry Branch Decorative Fence
Enlarge pattern 200%

BIRDHOUSE FENCE

Design by Bev Shenefield

This simple project adds a rustic focal point for your country garden.

CUTTING

1 Cut 2x2s into two 55-inch lengths (A), two 34½-inch lengths (B) and one 23-inch length (C).

2 Cut 1x4s into one 36-inch length (D), two 33-inch lengths (E), two 30-inch lengths (F) and two 27-inch lengths (G).

3 Cut a V point on one end of 23-inch 2x2 (C) and 55-inch 2x2s (A) to form stakes for inserting fence into ground.

4 Mark center top of one 27-inch 1x4 (G). On left side of board, mark 3 inches from top; use square to mark corresponding measurement on right side of board. Draw a line from left mark to center, and from right mark to center. Cut on lines for picket. Using this board as a pattern, mark and cut remaining 27-inch 1x4 (G), 36-inch 1x4 (D), both 33-inch 1x4s (E) and both 30-inch 1x4s (F) for pickets.

ASSEMBLE & FINISH

1 Referring to assembly diagram, use screws to fasten one 34½-inch 2x2 (B) to two 55-inch 2x2s (A) 23-inches up from the bottom; fasten remaining 34½-inch 2x2 (B) 18 inches above first; fasten 23-inch 2x2 (C) to center of lower 2x2 (B).

PROJECT SIZE
37½x55x2¼ inches, excluding birdhouses

TOOLS
- Power saw or handsaw
- Drill with bit to fit screws
- Square
- Mallet

SUPPLIES
- 2x2s: four 8-foot lengths
- 1x4s: five 5-foot lengths
- 3-inch galvanized screws
- 7D galvanized nails
- Exterior paint or stain: white and accent color
- Two 6½x6½x9-inch unfinished wooden birdhouses with removable roofs

2 Referring to assembly diagram, use nails to attach pickets (D, E, F and G) evenly spaced across 2x2 frame.

3 Remove birdhouse roofs. Apply white exterior paint or stain to fence and birdhouses; apply accent color paint or stain to birdhouse roofs. Let dry.

4 Use mallet to pound fence stakes into ground. Attach birdhouses to tops of 55-inch stakes with screws, then replace birdhouse roofs. ❋

BIRDHOUSE FENCE CUTTING CHART

P	T	W	L	#
A	2"	2"	55"	2
B	2"	2"	34½"	2
C	2"	2"	23"	1
D	1"	4"	36"	1
E	1"	4"	33"	2
F	1"	4"	30"	2
G	1"	4"	27"	2

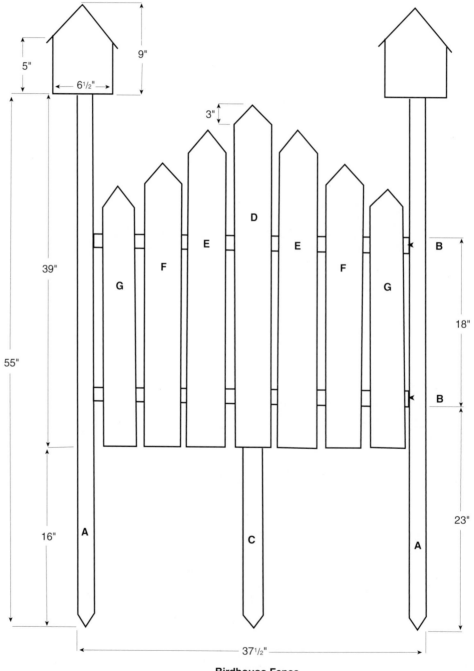

**Birdhouse Fence
Assembly Diagram**

DAISY BENCH

Design by Rue Ann Flanders

Every day will be bright and full of cheer when this decorates your yard! You can easily change the colors so the bench will match your favorite flowers.

CUTTING

1 For seat, use router and ¾-inch round over bit to round top edges of two 39-inch 1x4 boards (F) on both sides and ends; round bottom edges of each F piece on ends only. In same manner, round top edges of two 39-inch 1x2¹³⁄₁₆-inch boards (G) on both sides and ends; round bottom edges of each G piece on ends and one long side only. Sand edges smooth.

2 For skirt, round top edges of each 37½-inch 1x6 board (C) on one side and both ends. Sand edges smooth.

3 For legs, draw a horizontal line across each 16¼-inch 1x10-inch board (D) 8 inches from top; draw another line down vertical center of board. At bottom of each board, mark 3 inches in from each side. Draw a straight line from each

of these points to intersection of vertical and horizontal lines, forming a triangle. Cut out triangles using band saw or jigsaw. On each vertical line, drill and countersink a hole 2¼ inches and 4¾ inches from top edge. Sand edges smooth.

4 Cut each of three 10-inch 1x4 boards (A) to actual width of legs, for supports.

5 On each of six 2-inch 1x4 boards (B), drill and countersink two holes ½ inch from ends. These will be used as braces. ***Note:*** *Drill holes at a slight angle so drill will fit better when attaching braces to skirt.*

6 Using patterns provided, transfer daisy design onto 6x24x½-inch plywood with graphite paper; cut out with band saw or jigsaw. Using Dremel tool with a drum sanding attachment, round over curved edge of daisy center; mark center on the straight edge. Lightly sand edges of petals.

ASSEMBLE & FINISH

1 On each end of each support (A), glue one brace (B) at a 90-degree angle to support; let glue set. Turn support over and drill and countersink two screws from top of support into brace.

2 Stand one skirt piece (C) on long, unrounded edge; mark 1¾ inches from each end for attaching supports (A/B). Using 1¼-inch screws through predrilled holes, attach one end of each support to inside straight edge of skirt piece. Attach remaining support to inside straight edge of skirt centered between first two supports. Attach opposite ends of supports to remaining skirt piece. Leave assembled skirt upside down.

3 Position each leg (D) upside down between skirt pieces and against support. Measure 1¼ inches from each side of leg; drill and countersink a hole through leg and into support. Screw into place with 2-inch screws.

4 Place 33⅞x4¾x1-inch board (E) centered between the legs and resting on supports; drill two pilot holes through previously drilled holes on each leg into the ends of support. Screw into place with 2-inch screws. Stand bench upright. Drill and countersink two screws through each support into board E.

5 Place bench on its side. Mark center of front skirt for daisy design; lay out and trace daisy design onto skirt. ***Note:*** *Do not attach daisy at this time.* Following manufacturer's directions, stain all seat pieces (F and G) and eight flat wood plugs. Sand bench and fill the 4 holes on each leg with rounded wood plugs.

6 Using acrylic craft paint, paint all surfaces of bench skirt and legs, avoiding traced area for daisy placement; paint daisy center yellow and petals white; let dry. Glue daisy pieces in place; secure with clamps until dry.

7 Place seat pieces upside down on flat surface with two 4-inch pieces (F) in the middle, one 2¹³⁄₁₆-inch piece (G) on each side. Position bench upside down on top of seat so ends of seat overhang ends of skirt ¹¹⁄₁₆ inch, back of seat overhangs skirt by ⅝ inch, and front of seat overhangs daisy design by ⅝ inch; drill and countersink two holes through each support into each of two middle seat pieces (F). Secure with 1¼-inch screws.

PROJECT SIZE
39x12¾x17 inches

TOOLS
• Router with ¾-inch round over bit
• Band saw or jigsaw
• Drill with bit to fit screws, and countersink attachment
• Dremel tool with sanding drums

SUPPLIES
• Two 1x4x39-inch lengths
• Two 1x2¹³⁄₁₆x39-inch lengths
• Two 1x6x37½-inch lengths
• Two 1x10x16¼-inch lengths
• Three 1x4x10-inch lengths
• Six 1x2x4-inch pieces
• One 1x4¾x33⅞-inch length
• One 6x24x½-inch plywood
• Sandpaper
• Exterior wood glue
• Exterior wood screws: 1¼-inch, 2-inch
• ⅜-inch wood plugs: eight flat, four rounded
• Cherry wood stain
• Acrylic craft paint: yellow, white and green
• 4–6 clamps
• Exterior varnish

8 Turn bench upright and temporarily clamp two remaining seat pieces (G) in place. Drill and countersink two holes 2¼ inches from each end of each piece, with the first hole 2¼ inches from edge and the second hole 1½ inches from edge. Secure with 1¼-inch screws. Fill holes with prestained flat wood plugs.

9 If the bench is to be kept outdoors, finish with exterior varnish. ✿

DAISY BENCH CUTTING CHART

P	T	W	L	#
A	I"	4"	10"	3
B	I"	4"	2"	6
C	I"	6"	37½"	2
D	I"	10"	16¼"	2
E	I"	4¾"	33⅞"	1
F	I"	4"	39"	2
G	I"	2¹³⁄₁₆"	39"	2

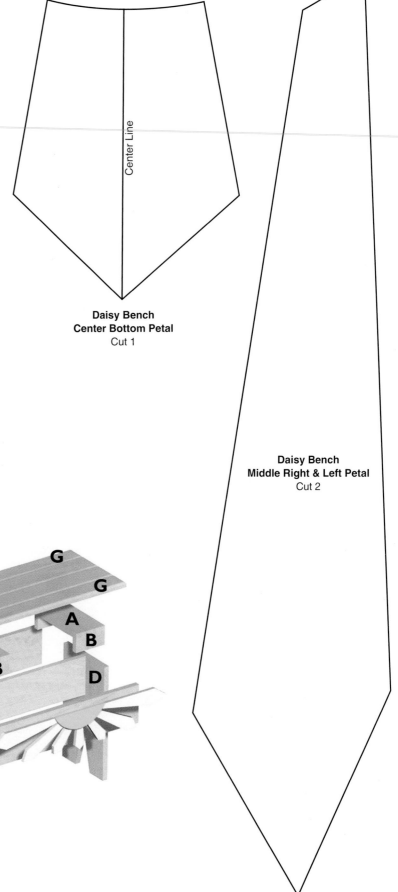

**Daisy Bench
Center Bottom Petal**
Cut 1

Center Line

**Daisy Bench
Middle Right & Left Petal**
Cut 2

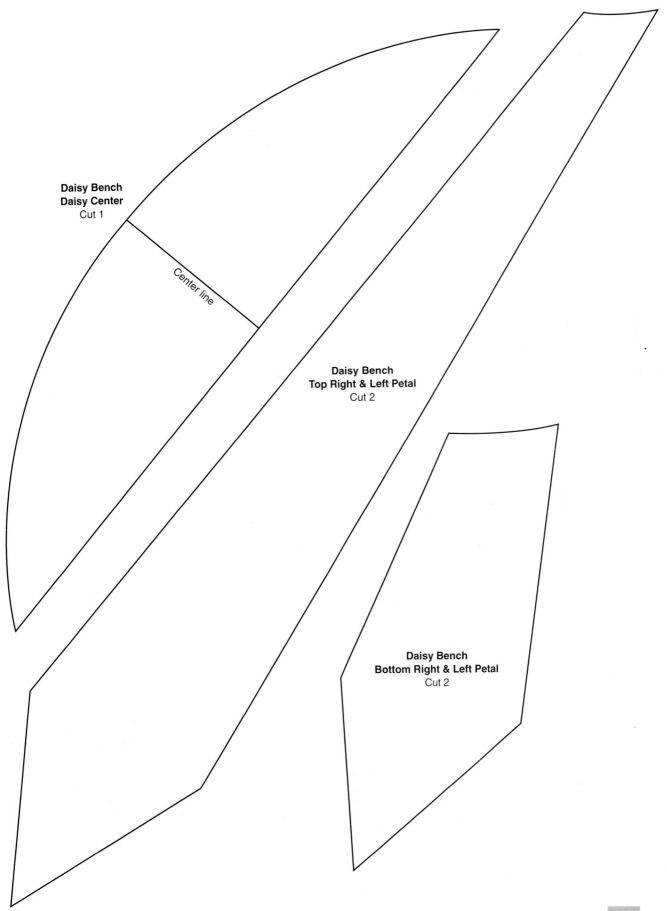

**Daisy Bench
Daisy Center**
Cut 1

Center line

**Daisy Bench
Top Right & Left Petal**
Cut 2

**Daisy Bench
Bottom Right & Left Petal**
Cut 2

SOUTHWESTERN-STYLE BENCH

Design by Johanna Johanson

Add a touch of the Southwest to your yard. Personalize it by choosing your own finish.

PROJECT NOTES

Cypress, pine, teak or redwood are recommended for this project.

Check boards carefully; reject any warped or split boards.

Bench could also be made using 4x4-inch stock lumber.

CUTTING

1 Cut 1x12 into one 40-inch length (A) for top, and two 15¼-inch lengths (C) for ends.

2 Cut 1x8 into two 40-inch lengths (B) for sides.

3 Referring to cutting diagrams, cut 1-inch-deep notches in both sides and ends.

ASSEMBLE & FINISH

1 On underside of top (A), draw a line across board 4 inches from each end to mark placement of ends.

2 On topside of top (A), draw a line across board 4⅜ inches from each end to mark screw placement.

Beginning and ending approximately 1 inch from each edge, use drill with $\frac{1}{16}$-inch bit to make three countersunk pilot holes evenly spaced across each line.

3 Lay top on one side. Place wood glue along the top edge of one end (B); align top edge of end with line on underside of the top. Clamp in place to dry, if needed.

4 Attach screws through top into ends. Use a damp cloth to remove excess glue. Attach opposite end (B) in same manner.

5 On top side of each side (C), draw a horizontal line across board $\frac{3}{8}$ inch from top edge and a vertical line $4\frac{1}{2}$ inches from each end to mark screw placement. On each side, make six countersunk pilot holes evenly spaced across top line and two additional holes evenly spaced across each end line. Glue and assemble sides to top and ends, clamping if needed. Remove excess glue with a damp cloth.

6 Following manufacturer's directions, fill screw holes with wood putty and sand. Paint bench as desired. ❋

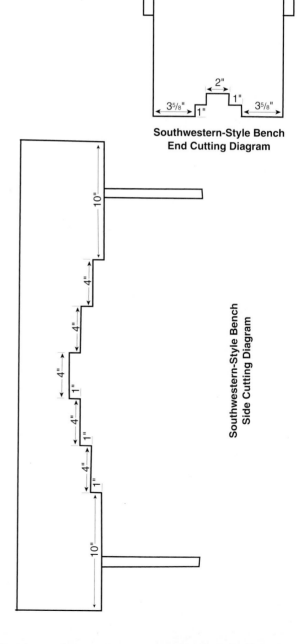

Southwestern-Style Bench End Cutting Diagram

Southwestern-Style Bench Side Cutting Diagram

PROJECT SIZE
40x16x12¾ inches

TOOLS
• Circular saw
• Band saw
• Drill with ¹⁄₁₆-inch drill bit, countersink attachment
• Square
• 4–6 clamps (optional)

SUPPLIES
• 1x6: one 8-foot board
• 1x8: one 8-foot board
• Square
• Exterior wood glue
• 4–6 clamps (optional)
• Thirty4–6 clamps (optional)
• Twenty-six 1½-inch #8 galvanized screws
• 80, 100, 150, 220 grit sSandpaper
• Wood putty (if painting bench)
• Putty knife
• Exterior stain, paint or marine varnish

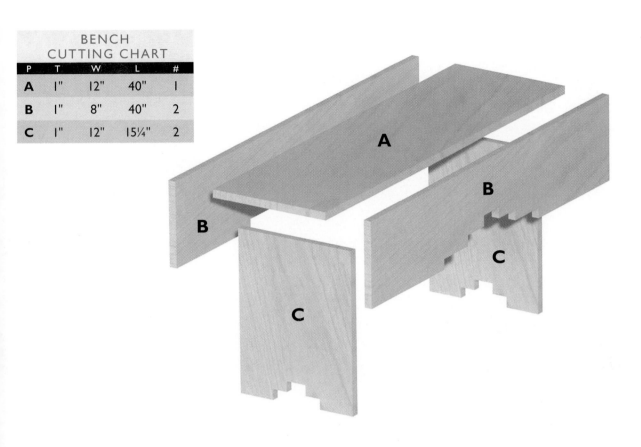

BENCH CUTTING CHART				
P	T	W	L	#
A	1"	12"	40"	1
B	1"	8"	40"	2
C	1"	12"	15¼"	2

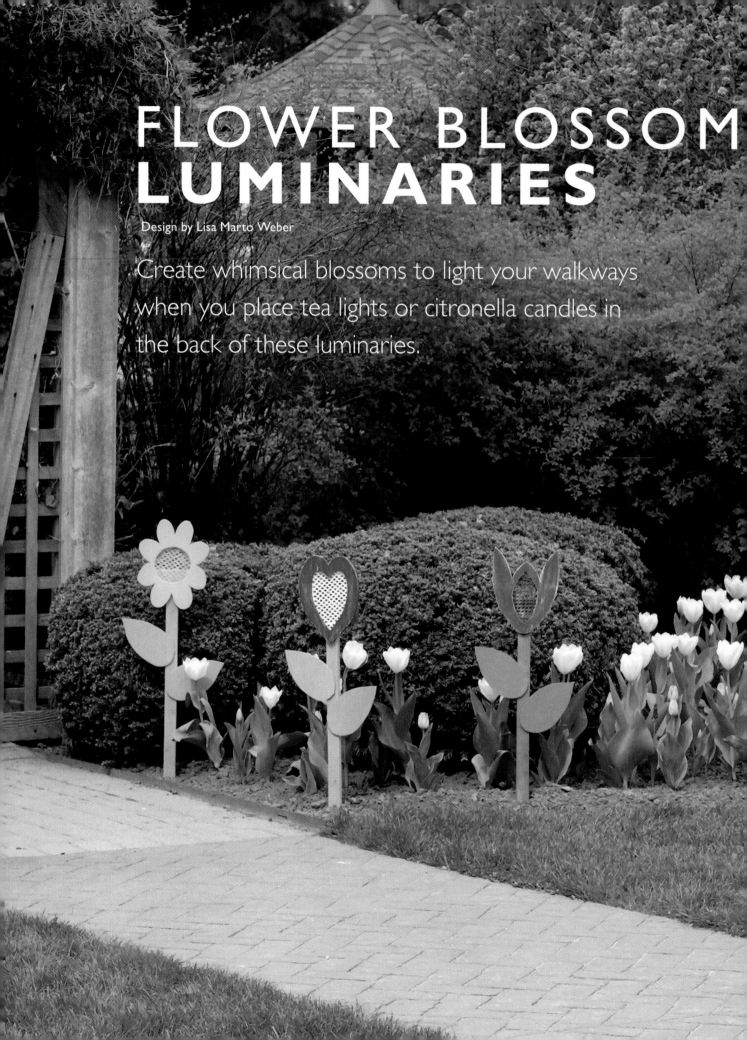

FLOWER BLOSSOM
LUMINARIES

Design by Lisa Marto Weber

Create whimsical blossoms to light your walkways
when you place tea lights or citronella candles in
the back of these luminaries.

CUTTING

1 Enlarge flower patterns for heart and tulip 115 percent; enlarge flower pattern for daisy 125 percent. Using jigsaw and enlarged patterns, cut each flower from ⅜-inch plywood. Cut two leaves for each flower from ³⁄₁₆-inch plywood. **Note:** *Use leaf pattern at original size.*

2 Drill a ½-inch pilot hole in center of each flower; cut out center using jigsaw.

3 With scroll saw, cut a V shape at the end of each 24-inch 1x2 for stakes. For each luminaire, cut each 20-inch 1x2 into two 4¼-inch and three 3-inch lengths.

4 For each flower, measure center opening; cut gutter guard or window screen slightly larger than center hole.

5 Sand all rough edges; remove dust with tack cloth.

ASSEMBLE & FINISH

1 For each candle base, glue and nail three 3-inch lengths togethe. Glue and nail two 4¼-inch pieces across bottom (see photos below).

2 Referring to photo for placement, glue and nail two leaves onto front of each stake. Paint stake and leaves green. **Note:** *For tulip and heart luminaires, paint top portions of stakes that show behind cutouts the same color as flower.*

3 Paint flower cutouts with red, purple and yellow; paint candle bases to match each flower. Paint gutter guard as desired. **Note:** *Gutter guard on sample projects was painted purple on purple luminaire and tan on yellow luminaire; it was left unpainted on red luminaire. If using window screen, do not paint.*

4 Glue gutter guard or window screen to back of each flower over center opening. Referring to patterns for placement, nail flowers onto stake fronts; nail candle bases onto flower backs (see photos on page 113). Fill nail holes with wood putty and sand following manufacturer's direction. Touch up filled holes with matching paint. Lightly sand flowers to create a rustic look. ❀

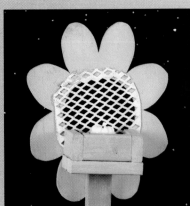
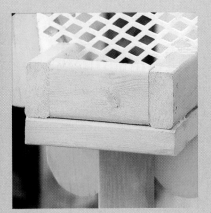

PROJECT SIZE
32x12x3¼

TOOLS
- Jigsaw
- Drill with ½-inch bit
- Scroll saw
- Nail gun with 1- and 1¾-inch nails, or hammer and 1-inch and 1¾-inch finish nails

SUPPLIES
- 1x2: three 24-inch lengths and three 20-inch lengths pine
- 35x17x⅜-inch plywood
- 30x12x³⁄₁₆-inch plywood
- 6-inch-wide white vinyl mesh gutter guard, or window screen
- Medium-grit sandpaper
- Tack cloth
- Multitask wood glue
- Acrylic paint: yellow, green, purple, red and tan
- 1-inch flat wash paintbrush
- Wood putty

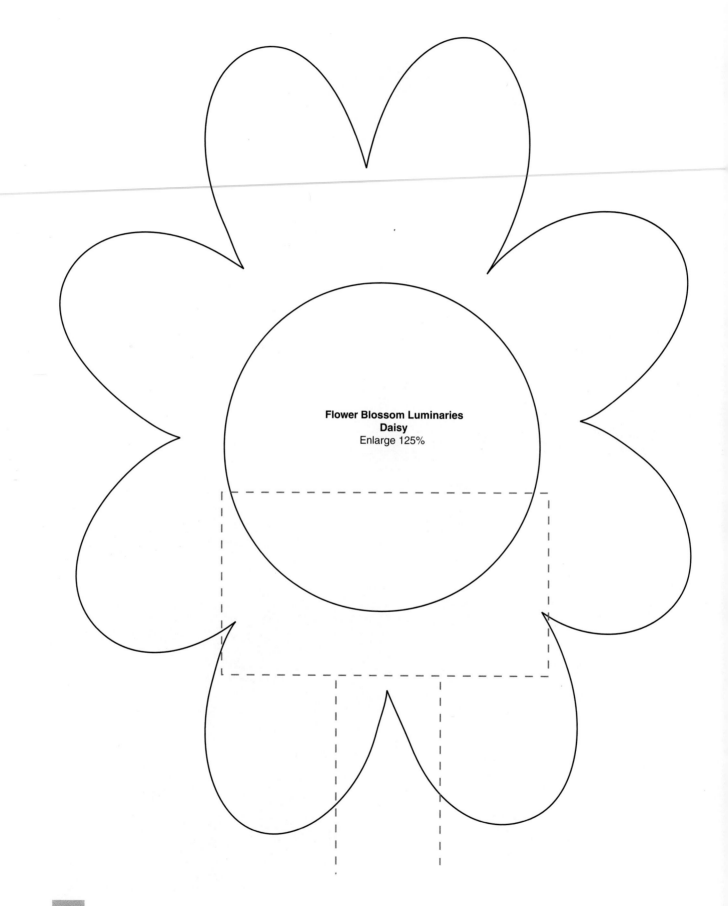

**Flower Blossom Luminaries
Daisy**
Enlarge 125%

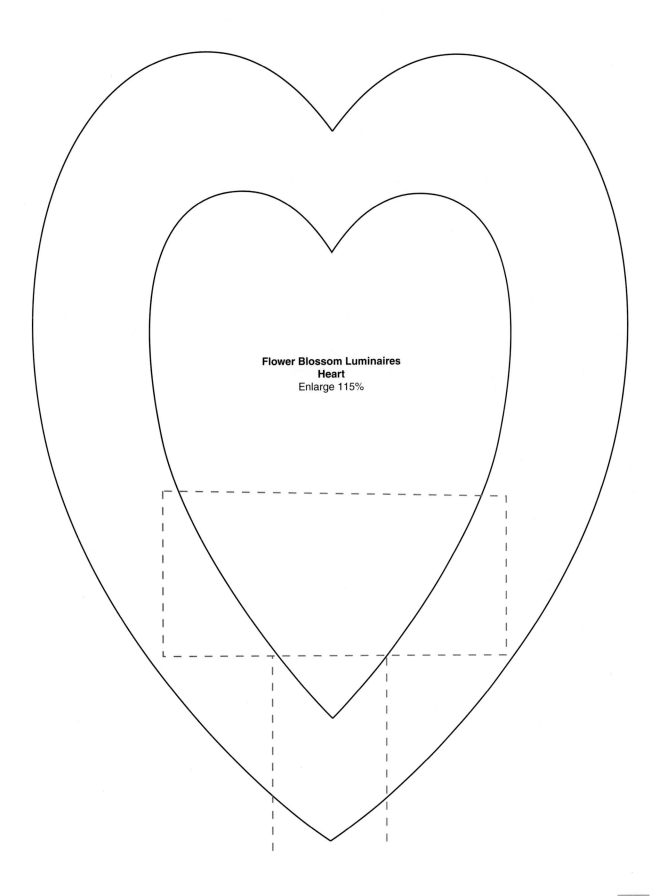

Flower Blossom Luminaires
Heart
Enlarge 115%

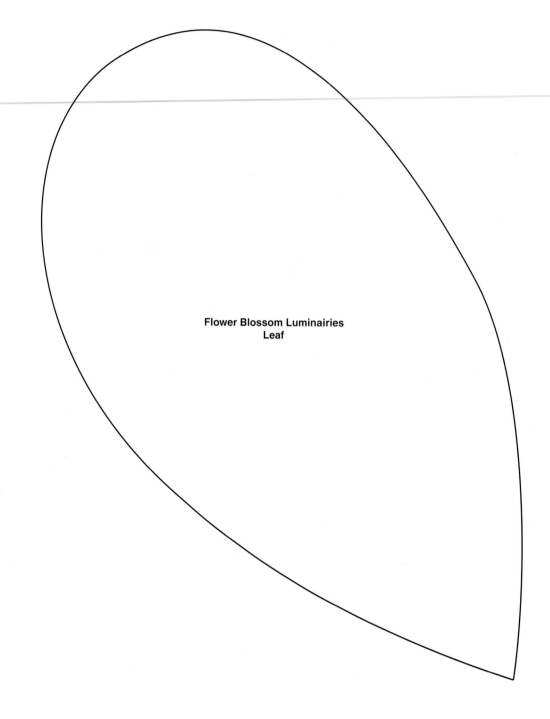

**Flower Blossom Luminairies
Leaf**

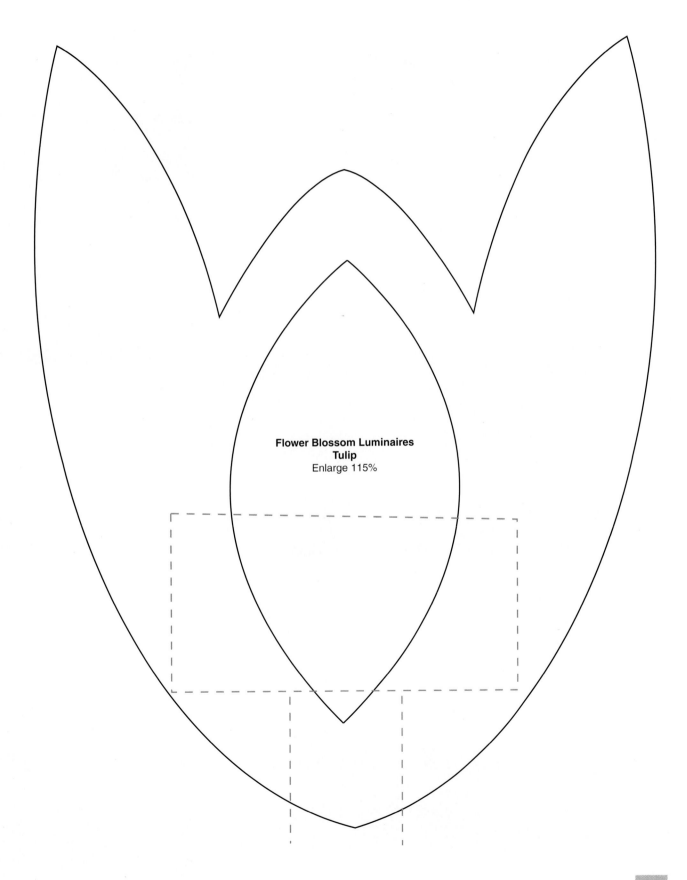

Flower Blossom Luminaires
Tulip
Enlarge 115%

CAT BIRDHOUSE

Design by Cindy Reusser

Your friends and neighbors will appreciate this humorous birdhouse, even if the birds don't! The back box portion of the birdhouse is built first, then the face is added.

CUTTING

1 Cut 1x5 into two 3½-inch lengths (A) for birdhouse top and bottom, and one 5-inch piece (C) for birdhouse back; cut 1x4 into two 3½-inch lengths (B) for birdhouse sides. Sand edges smooth.

2 Enlarge pattern for birdhouse front 115 percent. Use graphite paper to transfer outline of enlarged pattern to 9x8x1-inch board; cut out with scroll saw. Referring to pattern for placement, drill 1-inch hole for opening; drill ¼-inch hole for perch. Sand edges smooth.

ASSEMBLE & FINISH

1 Referring to assembly diagram, glue and nail birdhouse top and bottom (A) to birdhouse sides (B).

2 Place birdhouse back (C) over back of top, bottom and sides; drill a ⅛-inch hole at each corner. Attach back with galvanized screws.

3 Glue and nail birdhouse front to front of top, bottom and sides, making sure 1-inch opening is not obstructed by bottom of box.

4 Fill and sand all nail holes with wood putty following manufacturer's directions.

5 Base-coat cat face with cream; let dry. Transfer detail to face with graphite paper; paint as follows:

Outer ears and stripes around face and neck—paint with brown. **Face**—dry-brush with gold to shade; let dry. Shade and highlight with brown.

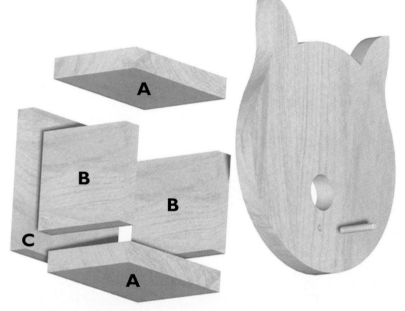

CAT BIRDHOUSE CUTTING CHART

P	T	W	L	#
A	1"	5"	3½"	2
B	1"	4"	3½"	2
C	1"	5"	5"	1

PROJECT SIZE
7¼x9x5 inches

TOOLS
- Scroll saw
- Drill with ⅛-, ¼- and 1-inch bits
- Phillips driver attachment, or Phillips head screwdriver
- Nail gun with 2-inch nails, or hammer and 2-inch finish nails

SUPPLIES
- 9x8x1-inch board
- 1x5: one 18-inch length
- 1x4: one 10-inch length
- ½ inch ¼-inch dowel
- Medium-grit sandpaper
- Graphite paper
- Exterior wood glue
- Four 1½-inch galvanized screws
- Wood putty
- Acrylic paint: cream, brown, black, gold, red
- ½-inch stencil brush
- Paintbrushes
- Antiquing gel
- Exterior finish
- Two eye screws
- 7 inches lightweight chain

Eyes—dot with black.
Nose—dry-brush with black.

6 Outline and add remaining detail with black; let dry. Using a dry stencil brush, blush cheek, mouth and nose area with barn red; let dry.

7 Following manufacturer's directions, apply antiquing gel to birdhouse front; let dry. Apply exterior finish to birdhouse front.

8 Insert eye screws in sides of birdhouse top; attach chain for hanging. ✳

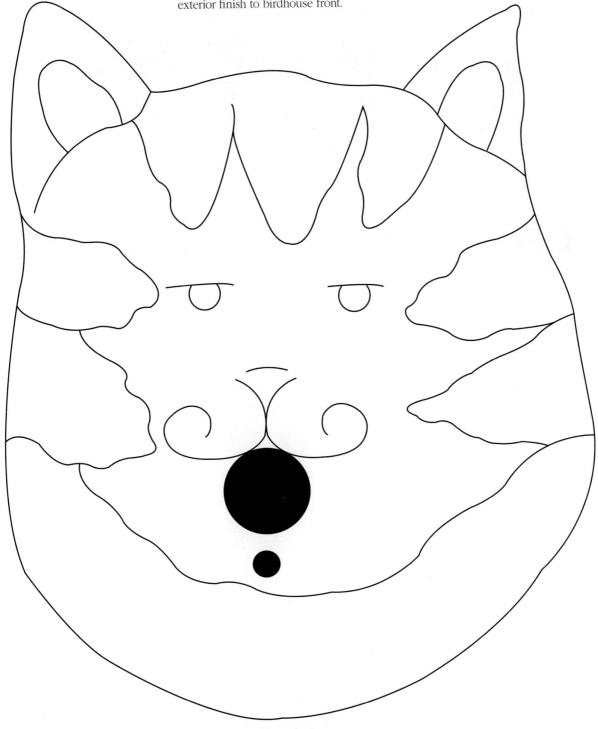

Cat Birdhouse
Front
Enlarge 115%

TREE EARRINGS

Design by Rue Ann Flanders

Creative Ideas for Yards & Gardens

Cut out these cute little earrings with your scroll saw and wear them wherever you go. Each piece is carefully cut out, painted, then glued together.

PROJECT NOTES

When painting, avoid traced areas for better glue adhesion when assembled.

Paint fronts and sides of all pieces; paint backs of large tree pieces only.

CUTTING

1 Cut two each large tree, small tree and trunk from ⅛-inch-thick Balsa wood.

2 Using 1/16-inch drill bit, drill a hole in large tree cutouts as indicated on pattern.

3 Sand lightly with 100-, 150- then 220-grit sandpaper; wipe clean.

PAINTING

1 Trace small tree onto each large tree cutout; trace trunk onto each small tree cutout.

2 Referring to project notes above, paint leaves on large tree dark green; paint leaves on small tree light green; paint trunk pieces and trunk portions of trees with brown. Let dry.

ASSEMBLE & FINISH

1 Use wood glue to glue pieces together; clamp until dry. If tree trunks do not align perfectly, sand to fit, then touch up with paint.

2 Add red dots as shown in photo; let dry.

3 Coat with semi-gloss finish; let dry.

4 Use small pliers to attach fishhook earring findings through holes. If preferred, attach ear clips to backs of large trees with two-part epoxy; let dry. ❋

PROJECT SIZE

1⁷⁄₁₆ x 1⁷⁄₁₆ inches, excluding earring findings

TOOLS

- Scroll saw
- Drill with ¹⁄₁₆-inch drill bit
- Small pliers

SUPPLIES

- ⅛-inch-thick Balsa wood
- 100-, 150-, 220-grit sandpaper
- Acrylic paint: dark green, light green, brown, red
- Wood glue
- Spring clamps
- Clear semi-gloss finish
- Two fishhook earring findings or ear clips
- Two-part epoxy (optional)

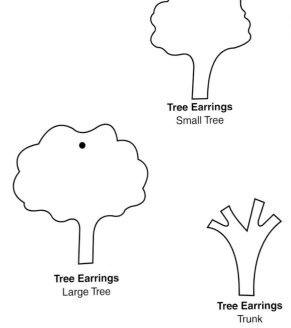

Tree Earrings
Small Tree

Tree Earrings
Large Tree

Tree Earrings
Trunk

POTTING TABLE

Design by Bev Shenefield

Country charm adds to the beauty of this easy-to-make, functional potting table.

CUTTING

1 Cut 2x4s into five 36-inch lengths (A), two 21-inch lengths (D), four 17-inch lengths (B) and four 33-inch lengths (C).

2 Cut 1x6s into, eight 60-inch lengths (F), two 57-inch lengths (G), two 54-inch lengths (H), two 51-inch lengths (I), nine 36-inch lengths (E), and twelve 5-inch lengths (J).

3 Mark center top of one 36-inch 1x6 (E). On left side of board, mark 3 inches from top; use square to mark corresponding measurement on right side of board. Draw a line from left mark to center, and from right mark to center. Cut on lines for picket. Using this board as a pattern, mark and cut remaining eight 36-inch 1x6s (E), eight 60-inch 1x6s (F), both 57-inch 1x6s (G), both 54-inch 1x6s (H) and both 51-inch 1x6s (I) for pickets.

4 Cut 7/16-inch dowel into four 3½-inch lengths. Lightly sand one end of each dowel.

ASSEMBLE & FINISH

1 Assemble frame according to pattern diagram using screws and exterior wood glue. Check frequently that all parts are square.

2 Nail four 36-inch 1x6s (E) on frame top, spacing evenly. Notch two 36-inch 1x6s (E) to fit frame for bottom shelf; nail into place. Add remaining two 36-inch 1x6s to complete bottom.

3 Referring to pattern, nail pickets (F, G, H and I) securely to back

and sides, spacing evenly. Add 5-inch
1x6s (J) across front edges, nailing
six across top and six across bottom.

4 Drill four 7/16-inch holes 1
inch from bottom edge of
remaining 36-inch 2x4 (A), spacing
approximately 7 inches apart. Glue
four dowels into holes.

5 Using nails or screws, level and
attach 2x4 with dowels to front
pickets of potting table approximately
10¾ inches from table top. Secure
remaining 36-inch 1x6 (E) to
attached 2x4 to form shelf.

6 Seal all exposed areas of potting
table with exterior stain or paint,
following manufacturer's directions.
Attach casters to bottom of table. ❀

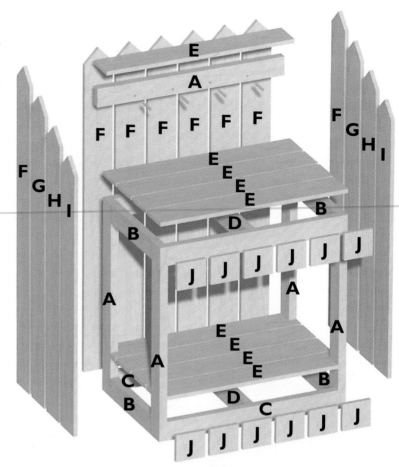

PROJECT SIZE
34½x18½x60 inches

TOOLS
• Power saw or handsaw
• Drill with 7/16-inch drill bit
• Square
• Level

SUPPLIES
• 2x4s: six 10-foot lengths pine or cedar
• 1x6s: twenty-five 6-foot lengths
   pine or cedar
• Fourteen inches 7/16-inch wooden dowel
• Sandpaper
• Exterior wood glue
• 3-inch #8 galvanized screws
• 2-inch galvanized nails
• Exterior stain or paint
• Four heavy-duty casters

POTTING TABLE CUTTING CHART

P	T	W	L	#
A	2"	4"	36"	5
B	2"	4"	17"	4
C	2"	4"	33"	4
D	2"	4"	21"	2
E	1"	6"	36"	9
F	1"	6"	60"	8
G	1"	6"	57"	2
H	1"	6"	54"	2
I	1"	6"	51"	2
J	1"	6"	5"	12

GOLDEN STAR WIND CHIME

Design by Lisa Marto Weber

When the wind blows these delightful chimes, you won't need to catch a falling star. Use your scroll saw to notch the stars and hold them together.

CUTTING

1 Using patterns provided, trace two small, one medium, one large and one extra-large star onto plywood; cut out using scroll saw.

2 Make a 1½-inch-long x ⅛-inch-wide notch on center bottom of each medium and large star between two points. ***Note:*** *A scrap of ⅛-inch-thick plywood is a useful guide.* Cut out with scroll saw.

3 Drill a hole approximately 1 inch from each tip of one small star and one hole in center of same star (for bottom star); drill a hole in center of remaining small star (for top star), in top point of medium star and in center bottom of extra-large star. Sand smooth; wipe with tack cloth.

ASSEMBLE & FINISH

1 Stain all stars with oak stain using a soft cloth; let dry.

2 Referring to photo, glue top point of large star into notch on bottom of medium star; glue top point of extra-large star into notch on bottom of large star; let dry.

3 Use nylon monofilament to attach chimes to bottom small star through drilled holes; adjust hanging length and secure ends on top of star.

4 Thread another length of nylon monofilament through hole in center bottom of extra-large star; thread ends through center hole in top small star, then through center hole in bottom small star; knot ends securely. Glue small stars together with wood hot-glue.

5 Thread another length of nylon monofilament through hole in top point of medium star; knot ends together for hanger. ✿

PROJECT SIZE
Approximately 6x28 inches, excluding hanger

TOOLS
- Scroll saw
- Hand drill with $\frac{1}{8}$-inch bit

SUPPLIES
- 20x20x$\frac{1}{8}$-inch birch plywood
- Sandpaper
- Tack cloth
- Oak stain
- Soft cloth
- Aleene's wood glue
- Nylon monofilament
- Five gold-finish $\frac{7}{16}$-inch tubular chimes ranging from 8–12 inches
- Hot-glue gun with wood-glue sticks

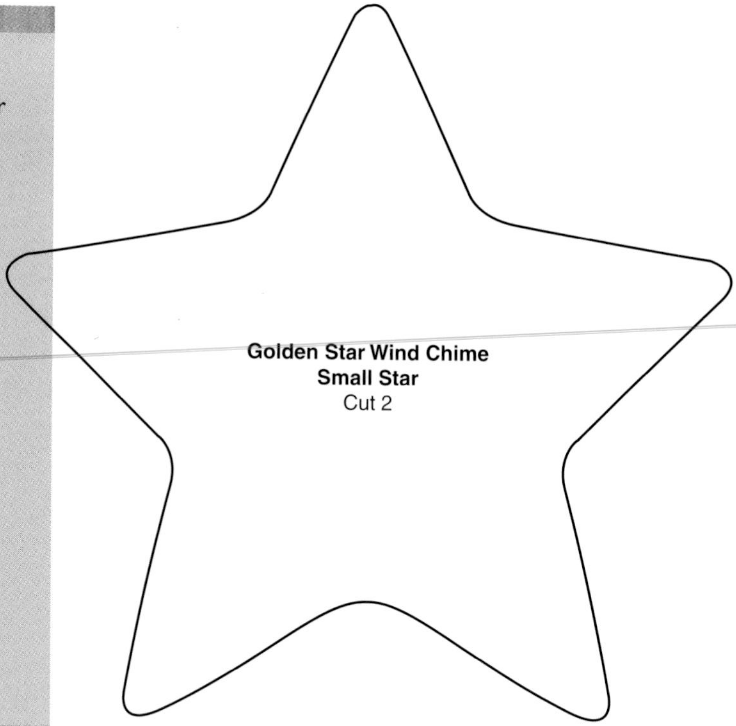

Golden Star Wind Chime
Small Star
Cut 2

Golden Star Wind Chime
Large Star
Cut 1

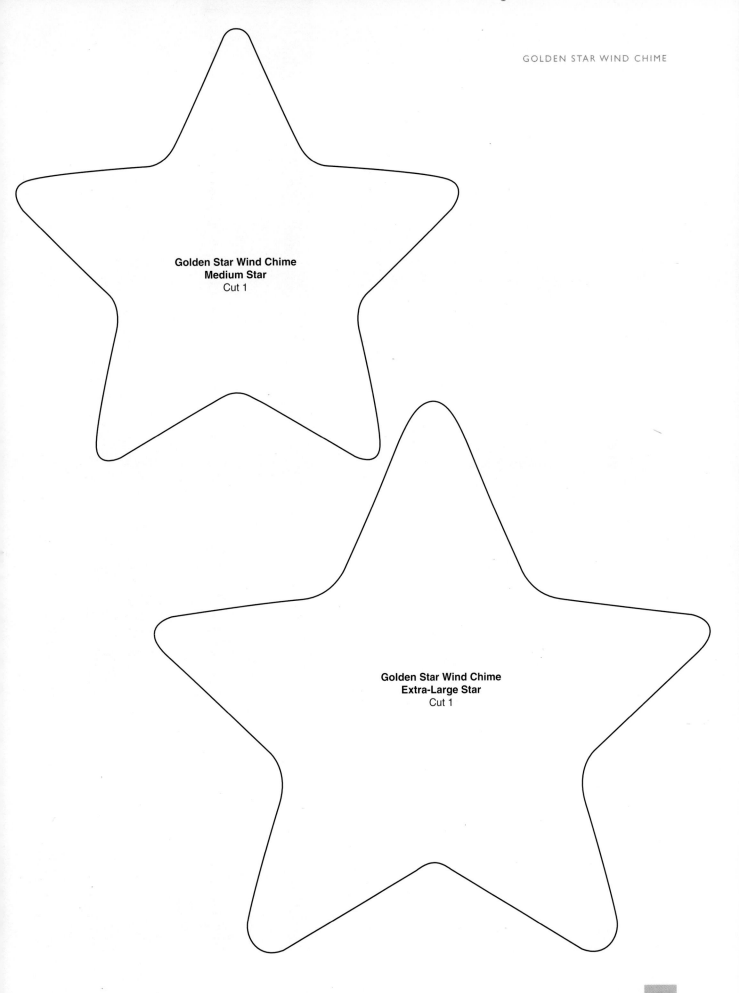

Golden Star Wind Chime
Medium Star
Cut 1

Golden Star Wind Chime
Extra-Large Star
Cut 1

Gardens

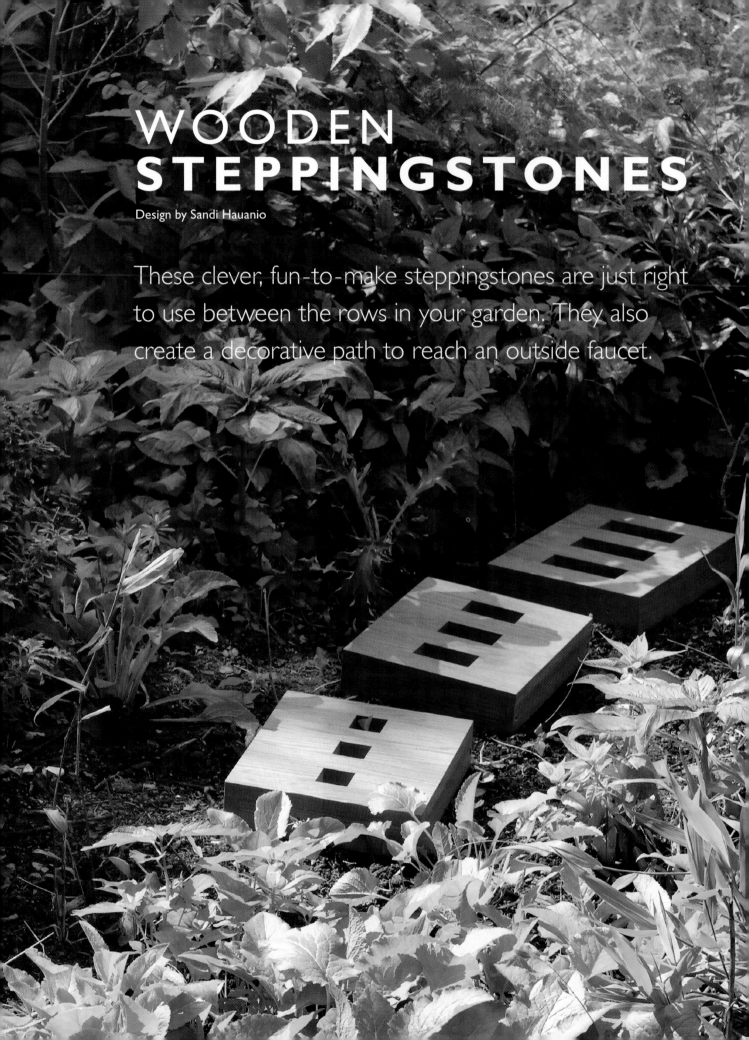

WOODEN STEPPINGSTONES

Design by Sandi Hauanio

These clever, fun-to-make steppingstones are just right to use between the rows in your garden. They also create a decorative path to reach an outside faucet.

PROJECT NOTE

Cedar is also suitable for this project.

CUTTING

1 Cut 1x2 into six 10½-inch lengths (A), eighteen 9-inch lengths (C), six 7½-inch lengths (B), six 3¾-inch lengths (D), six 3-inch lengths (E) and six 2¼-inch lengths (F).

ASSEMBLE & FINISH

Note: Slats are secured by drilling and countersinking pilot holes through bottom of frame and inner supports.

Frame

1 Referring to Fig. 1, form a rectangle with two 10½-inch pieces (A) and two 7½-inch pieces (B). Drill and countersink a pilot hole at each corner; drive in screws to secure.

2 Repeat step 1 to make two additional frames.

Stone No. 1

1 For inner supports, place two 9-inch pieces (C) within frame 2¼ inches from sides (Fig. 2). Secure supports to ends of frame by drilling and countersinking a pilot hole at each end of supports; drive in screws.

2 Place another 9-inch piece (C) across one end of frame with edges flush; clamp in place. Flip frame over; secure with two screws (Fig. 3). Repeat at opposite end of frame.

3 In same manner, clamp and secure to frame six 3¾-inch pieces (D) and two more 9-inch pieces (C) in alternate rows (Figs. 4a and 4b).

Stone No. 2

1 Repeat step 1 of Stone No. 1, positioning inner supports 1¾ inches from sides.

2 Complete as for Stone No. 1, using four 9-inch pieces (C) and six 3-inch pieces (E).

Stone No. 3

1 Repeat step 1 of Stone No. 1, positioning inner supports ⅞ inches from sides.

PROJECT SIZE
8¾x10¼x2⅛ inches

TOOLS
• Miter saw, or hand saw and miter box
• Drill
• Countersink bit with drill bit for pilot holes
• Four clamps

SUPPLIES
• 1x2: 28 feet redwood
• 1¾-inch exterior wood screws

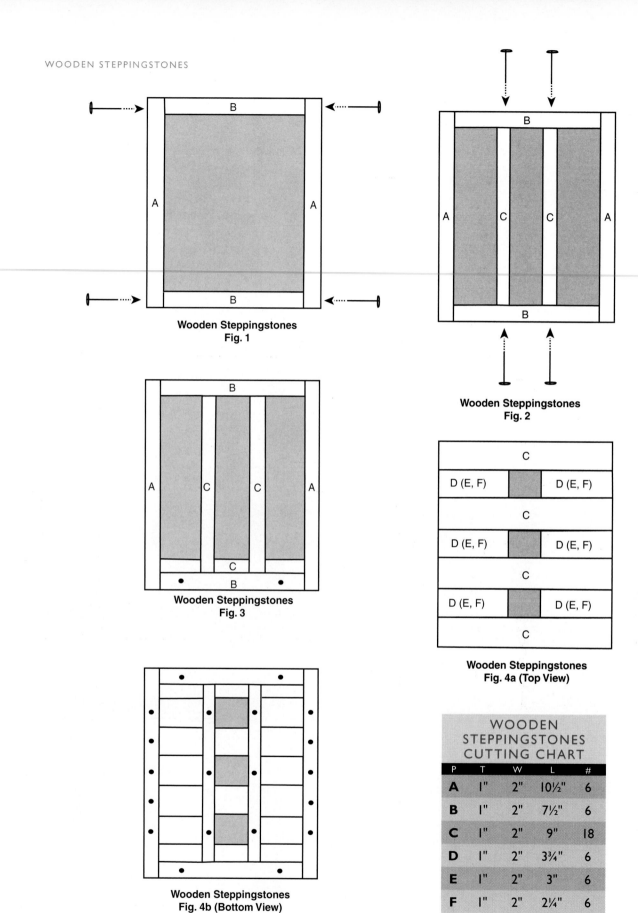

Wooden Steppingstones
Fig. 1

Wooden Steppingstones
Fig. 2

Wooden Steppingstones
Fig. 3

Wooden Steppingstones
Fig. 4a (Top View)

Wooden Steppingstones
Fig. 4b (Bottom View)

WOODEN STEPPINGSTONES CUTTING CHART

P	T	W	L	#
A	1"	2"	10½"	6
B	1"	2"	7½"	6
C	1"	2"	9"	18
D	1"	2"	3¾"	6
E	1"	2"	3"	6
F	1"	2"	2¼"	6

LOG CABIN
STEPPINGSTONE

Design by Sandi Hauanio

Add a rustic touch to your garden with this
easy-to-make steppingstone.

PROJECT NOTE

Cedar is also suitable for this project.

CUTTING

1 Cut 1x2 into two 10½-inch lengths (A), six 9¾-inch lengths (B), two 9-inch lengths (E), two 6¾-inch lengths (F), two 6-inch lengths (G), two 3¾-inch lengths (H), two 3-inch lengths (I) and two 1½-inch lengths (C).

2 Cut 2x2 into four 9¾-inch lengths (D).

ASSEMBLE & FINISH

Note: Slats are secured by drilling and countersinking pilot holes through bottom of frame and inner supports.

1 Referring to Fig. 1, form a rectangle with two 10½-inch pieces (A) and two 9¾-inch pieces (B). Drill and countersink a pilot hole at each corner; drive in screws to secure.

2 For center supports (Fig. 2), place two more 9¾-inch pieces (B) inside frame 3 inches from each side. Secure center supports to ends of frame by drilling and countersinking a pilot hole at each end of supports; drive in screws. Nail 1½-inch pieces (C) between center supports 3 inches from top and bottom.

3 For side supports, place two 9¾-inch 2x2s (D) on each side of center supports; secure at sides and ends of frame (Fig. 3).

4 Place another 9¾-inch piece (B) flush with one long side of frame and with one end of frame, leaving a 1½-inch space at end; clamp in place. Flip frame over; secure with three screws.

5 Referring to assembly diagram, attach remaining slats, working from outer edge to center. ❀

LOG CABIN STEPPINGSTONES CUTTING CHART				
P	T	W	L	#
A	1"	2"	10½"	2
B	1"	2"	9¾"	6
C	1"	2"	1½"	2
D	2"	2"	9¾"	4
E	1"	2"	9"	2
F	1"	2"	6¾"	2
G	1"	2"	6"	2
H	1"	2"	3¾"	2
I	1"	2"	3"	2

PROJECT SIZE
10½x11¼x2⅛ inches

TOOLS
- Miter saw, or hand saw and miter box
- Drill
- Countersink bit with drill bit for pilot holes
- Four clamps

SUPPLIES
- 1x2: 15 feet redwood
- 2x2: 4 feet cedar
- ½-inch finish nails
- 1¼-inch exterior wood screws
- 1¾-inch exterior wood screws

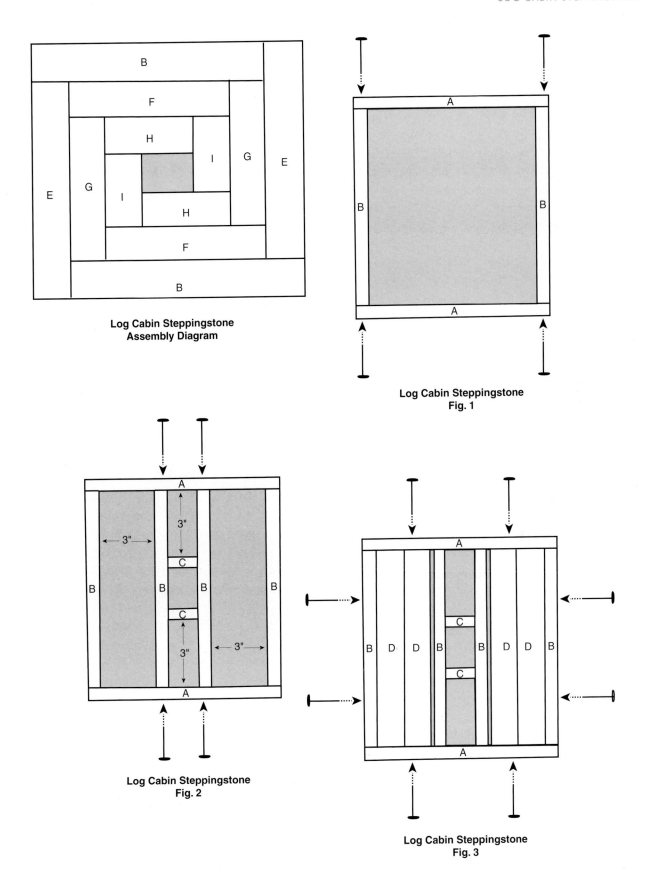

Log Cabin Steppingstone
Assembly Diagram

Log Cabin Steppingstone
Fig. 1

Log Cabin Steppingstone
Fig. 2

Log Cabin Steppingstone
Fig. 3

PEEK-A-BOO STEPPINGSTONES

Design by Sandi Hauanio

Place these steppingstones in the center of your flower bed to have a decorative place to stand when gardening.

PROJECT NOTE
Cedar is also suitable for this project.

CUTTING

1 Cut 1x2 into four 10½-inch lengths (A), sixteen 9-inch lengths (C), four 7½-inch lengths (B), two 6-inch lengths (D), four 4½-inch lengths (F) and six 1½-inch lengths (E).

ASSEMBLE & FINISH
Note: Slats are secured by drilling and countersinking pilot holes through bottom of frame and inner supports.

Frame

1 Referring to Fig. 1, form a rectangle with two 10½-inch pieces (A) and two 7½-inch pieces (B). Drill and countersink a pilot hole at each corner; drive in screws to secure.

2 Repeat step 1 to make one additional frame.

Stone No. 1

1 For side supports, place two 9-inch pieces (C) within frame

along each side (Fig. 2); glue and nail to sides of frame from inside.

2 For inner support, glue two 9-inch pieces (C) together; clamp until dry. Place inner support inside frame 3⅛ inches from left side support. Secure inner support to ends of frame by drilling and countersinking a pilot hole at each end of support; drive in screws (Fig. 3).

3 Place another 9-inch piece (C) across one end of frame with edges flush; clamp in place. Flip frame over; secure with two screws (Fig. 4). Repeat at opposite end of frame.

4 Referring to assembly diagram for Stone No. 1, attach in same manner two more 9-inch slats (C), one 6-inch slat (D), three 1½-inch slats (E) and two 4½-inch slats (F), securing slats with one screw at each end. *Note: Secure 1½-inch slats with one screw only.*

Stone No. 2

1 Repeat step 1 of Stone No. 1; turn frame so 3⅛-inch opening is on right side.

2 Referring to assembly diagram for Stone No. 2, complete as for Stone No. 1, reversing positions of F and E slats, and D and E slats. ✿

PROJECT SIZE

8¾x10¼x2⅛ inches

TOOLS

- Miter saw, or hand saw and miter box
- Drill
- Countersink bit with drill bit for pilot holes
- Four clamps

SUPPLIES

- 1x2: 22 feet redwood
- 1¾-inch exterior wood screws
- Wood glue
- 1-inch finish nails

PEEK-A-BOO STEPPPINGSTONES CUTTING CHART				
P	T	W	L	#
A	1"	2"	10½"	4
B	1"	2"	7½"	4
C	1"	2"	9"	16
D	1"	2"	6"	2
E	1"	2"	1½"	6
F	1"	2"	4½"	4

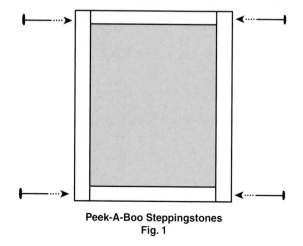

**Peek-A-Boo Steppingstones
Fig. 1**

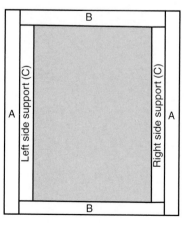

**Peek-A-Boo Steppingstones
Fig. 2**

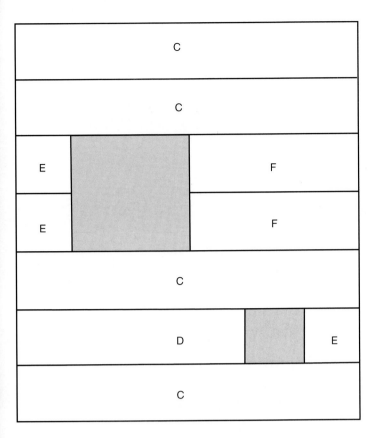

Peek-A-Boo Steppingstones
Assembly Diagram
Stone No. 1

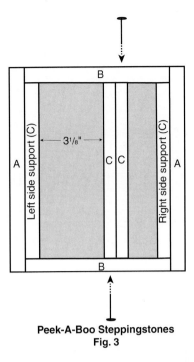

Peek-A-Boo Steppingstones
Fig. 3

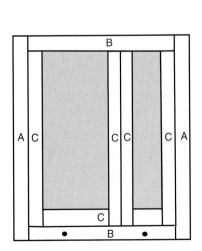

Peed-A-Boo Steppingstones
Fig. 4

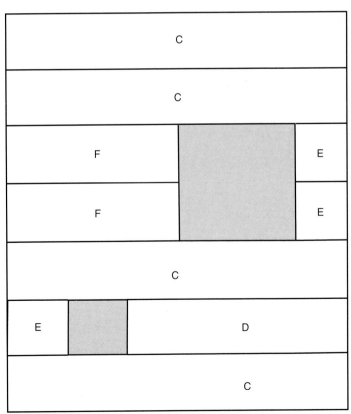

Peek-A-Boo Steppingstones
Assembly Diagram
Stone No. 2

STENCIL IN RELIEF GARDEN SIGN

Design by Barbara Greve

Relief stenciling adds a new dimension to this charming sign. Welcome guests to your own secret garden.

PROJECT NOTES

Let paint dry between coats.

To dry-brush, load the brush with paint then rub most of it off on a paper towel; scrub the remaining color onto the area to be painted.

INSTRUCTIONS

1 Sand edges of board smooth; remove dust with a damp paper towel. Let dry. Spray entire surface with sealer; let dry.

2 Draw a horizontal line across board 4 inches from bottom edge; draw a vertical line 1¾ inches from left side of board.

3 Cut alphabet stencil apart leaving a ¼-inch border around each letter. Position letters on the horizontal line, spacing approximately ½-inch apart. Carefully lift each stencil and apply spray stencil adhesive to back, then reposition. Position rose stencils around lettering as desired.

4 Using palette knife, cover a letter with decorative snow, then carefully lift stencil to remove. Repeat to cover all letters and roses. Use fingertip dipped in water to smooth over letters where needed, leaving some unevenness to add interest. Let dry completely.

5 Paint entire board with dark green. Following manufacturer's directions, apply crackle medium over green; let dry. Paint entire board again with ivory; let dry completely.

6 Using photo as a guide, dry-brush stenciled design as follows:
Top right rose, top left bud and second rose on bottom left cluster—rose.
Left rose on bottom left cluster and left rose on bottom right—tan.
Remaining roses—pink.
Sky—Use the following: mix one part cornflower blue and one part white, then mix one part blue/white mixture with one part sky blue.
Around all leaves and flowers—light green.
Leaves and stems—dark green.

7 Paint lettering using a #2 pointed round brush and English yew green, holding brush horizontally over letters while painting to allow pockets of light ivory to show through. Let dry overnight.

8 Following manufacturer's directions, apply two coats of matte exterior/interior varnish to entire surface of sign.

9 Drill a ¹⁄₁₆-inch hole in top edge of sign 1½ inches from each side. Screw ⅜-inch eye screw into each hole. With needle-nose pliers, open a link on each end of the chain; slip opened links over eye screws, then press link closed again. ❁

TOOLS

- Drill with 1/16-inch bit
- Needle-nose pliers

SUPPLIES

- 15¼x9¼x1-inch pine board
- Fine-grit sandpaper
- Spray sealer
- Stencil Magic stencils from Delta: 2-inch
  Olde English Alphabet #95 624 0018
  and Rose Border #95 127 0018
- Spray stencil adhesive
- Decorative snow paint
- Palette knife
- Acrylic paint: Dark green, ivory, rose, pink,
  tan, white, cornflower blue, light green,
  sky blue
- Paintbrushes, including a #2 pointed round
- Paint palette
- Crackle medium
- Matte exterior/interior varnish
- Two 3/8-inch eye screws
- 14 inches ¼-inch chain
- Paper towels

HOW TO STENCIL IN RELIEF

Design by Barbara Greve

Apply a creative technique to achieve a 3-D image. Use the technique that you have learned to create a sign for your garden.

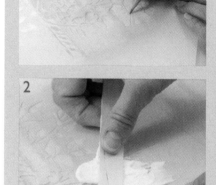

PROJECT NOTE

If using alphabet stencils, cut each letter apart leaving a ¼-inch margin. Other stencils can be used in whole or in part.

INSTRUCTIONS

1 Position stencils on plaque or board and mark with pencil. Remove each stencil and spray lightly with stencil adhesive, then reposition where marked (Photo 1).

2 Using a palette knife, completely cover cut out area of stencil with decorative snow (Photo 2).

3 Smooth the entire area with the palette knife, making it as even as possible (Photo 3).

4 With fingernail, gently lift edge of stencil; continue to lift slowly to remove (Photo 4).

5 Moisten a finger in water and smooth over decorative snow as desired (Photo 5).

6 Allow decorative snow to dry thoroughly. Paint and finish as desired. ❋

SUPPLIES
- Pine board or surface of choice
- Pencil
- Stencil of choice
- Spray stencil adhesive
- Decorative snow paint
- Palette knife
- Water

PAINTED GARDEN TABLE

Design by Sandi Hauanio

Lounge beside your garden, drink some freshly squeezed lemonade and admire your handiwork. This table is a great size for a side table by a lawn chair, or to hold supplies clearly in sight when you are gardening.

CUTTING

1 Cut 2x2 into four 13½-inch lengths (A) for legs.

2 Cut 1x3 into four 15-inch lengths (F) for top tabletop frame, and four 13½-inch lengths (E) for bottom tabletop frame.

3 Cut 1x2 into four 10½-inch lengths (D) for center vertical slats, eight 11¼-inch lengths (C) for outer vertical slats, ten 12-inch lengths (B) for horizontal slats, and six 9-inch lengths (G) for tabletop slats.

SIDES

1 With pencil, mark top of each leg (A) 1½ inches from end.

2 Place two legs on flat surface; place one 12-inch horizontal slat (B) across legs just below pencil line. Adjust legs so sides of legs are flush with each end of horizontal

slat. Clamp ends to hold in place and drill and countersink a hole on top of each end of slat into leg. Remove one clamp and screw into slat, then repeat on opposite leg.

3 Place another horizontal slat (B) next to first slat and clamp in place; draw a pencil line below second slat to mark placement of next slat, then remove clamped slat. Attach next horizontal slat in place just below pencil line as for first slat. Repeat step 3 for third slat.

4 Repeat steps 2 and 3 for second side A.

5 Stand both sides A upright on flat surface facing each other, approximately 12 inches apart, with horizontal slats on inside.

6 Slide four remaining 12-inch slats (B) into place (Fig. 1); clamp at eight points, making sure ends of slats are flush with outer edges of legs. Drill and countersink a hole at each point and drive screw into leg.

VERTICAL SLATS

1 Place table on one side. Mark top of four 11¼-inch outer slats (C)

¾ inch from one end. Referring to Fig. 2, place two slats on side A 1½ inches from each leg, aligning pencil mark with top edge of top slat; drill and countersink three holes in each vertical slat and drive screws. Repeat on opposite side A.

2 Mark top of remaining four 11¼-inch outer slats (C) 2 inches from one end. Referring to Fig. 3, attach to sides B in same manner as in step 1.

3 Mark top of two 10½-inch center slats (D) 1½-inches from one end; Referring to Fig. 4, attach to sides A as for outer vertical slats.

4 Repeat step 3 with remaining two 10½-inch center slats (D), marking tops 3 inches from ends (Fig. 5). **Note:** *Before securing, make sure center slat does not sit higher than tops of legs.*

5 Fill and sand all drilled holes with wood putty following manufacturer's directions. Sand sides; finish with exterior primer and paint.

TABLETOP

1 Referring to Fig. 6, miter ends of each 13½-inch bottom frame

piece (E) and 15-inch top frame piece (F). Glue and clamp with web clamp. Let dry.

2 With pencil, mark ¾ inch from outer edge on each side of top frame. Place bottom frame on top frame, aligning edges with pencil lines. Glue and clamp into place. Let dry.

3 Line up six 9-inch tabletop slats (G) side by side on flat surface. Flip tabletop over and fit over slats. Drill and countersink holes at each end of slat into bottom frame; drive screws to secure.

4 With pencil, mark ¾ inch from outer edge on each side of bottom frame. Flip tabletop right side up and place on sides, positioning legs inside pencil marks. Drill and countersink one hole per leg; drive screws to secure.

5 Fill and sand drilled holes with wood putty following manufacturer's directions. Sand tabletop; finish with exterior primer and paint. Let dry. ✸

PROJECT SIZE
15x15x15¼ inches

TOOLS
- Miter saw, or hand saw with miter box
- Drill
- Countersink bit with drill bit for pilot hole
- Web clamp
- 2–4 bar clamps or C-clamps

SUPPLIES
- 2x2: 6 feet
- 1x3: 10 feet
- 1x2: 28 feet
- Sixty 1¼-inch exterior wood screws
- Wood putty
- Sandpaper
- Exterior primer and paint
- Exterior wood glue

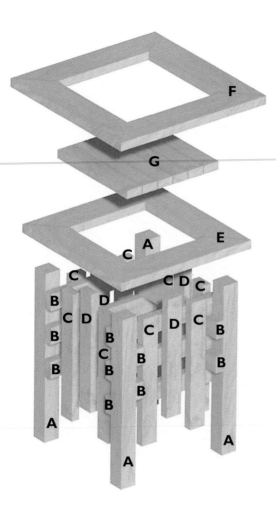

PAINTED GARDEN TABLE CUTTING CHART

P	T	W	L	#
A	2"	2"	13½"	4
B	1"	2"	12"	10
C	1"	2"	11¼"	8
D	1"	2"	10½"	4
E	1"	3"	13½"	4
F	1"	3"	15"	4
G	1"	2"	9"	6

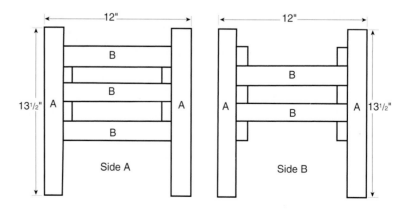

Painted Garden Table
Fig. 1

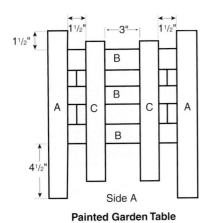

**Painted Garden Table
Fig. 2**

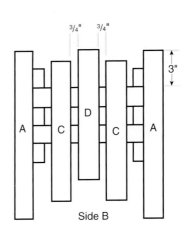

**Painted Garden Table
Fig. 3**

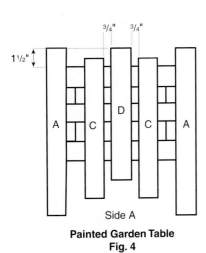

**Painted Garden Table
Fig. 4**

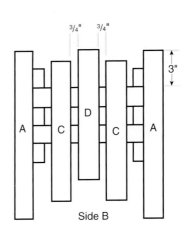

**Painted Garden Table
Fig. 5**

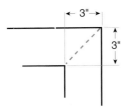

**Painted Garden Table
Fig. 6**

IVY POTTING TABLE

Design by Rue Ann Flanders

Add elegance and sophistication to your garden with a lovely potting table. It will inspire you to be creative in both woodworking and gardening.

PROJECT NOTE

Carefully check framing studs for warping before purchasing.

CUTTING

1 Cut 2x6 framing studs into four 27-inch lengths (D). For legs, place all four 27-inch 2x6s (D) on flat surface. Separate two for the left legs and two for the right legs. Referring to Fig. 1, notch legs to accommodate 25-inch 2x4 table braces (E).

2 Cut 2x4 framing studs into one 46½-inch (B), six 46½-inch lengths (G), six 39½-inch lengths (A), four 25-inch lengths (E), two 24⅝-inch lengths (C) and two 5½-inch lengths (P).

3 For tabletop frame, miter both ends of one 46½-inch 2x4 (B) at a 45-degree angle; miter one end of each 24⅝-inch 2x4 (C).

4 Cut 2x2 framing studs into two 21¾-inch lengths (F) and four 4-inch lengths (H).

5 Cut poplar 1x6 into two 48-inch lengths (I and O), three 46½-inch lengths (J, K and L), two 25-inch lengths (N) and two 20½-inch lengths (M).

6 Cut planed 84-inch 1x6 into six 14-inch lengths. Enlarge ivy patterns 153 percent; transfer as desired onto planed 14-inch lengths and cut out using scroll saw; sand edges. *Note: Sample project used Ivy A on top back and Ivy B on remaining pieces.*

7 Enlarge patterns for top back and shelf skirt 132 percent; assemble pattern pieces as indicated. Transfer pattern for top back onto one 48-inch 1x6 (I), aligning center line of

pattern with center of board; flip pattern to opposite side (aligning centers) and transfer remaining half of design. In same manner, transfer pattern for shelf skirt onto one 46½-inch 1x6 (J). Cut out using scroll saw or jigsaw; sand edges. Using router with round over bit, round over front curved edge of top back; round over front curved and straight edges of shelf skirt.

8 For top shelf unit, use router with round over bit to route both edges of one long side of one 46½-inch 1x6 (K) for top shelf; route both edges of one long side of each 20½-inch 1x6 (M) for shelf sides. *Note: Routed edges will be fronts.* Rip cut remaining 46½-inch 1x6 (L) to 4⅞ inches wide for middle shelf. Referring to Fig. 2, draw a curve on one end of each 5⅛-inch 2x4 for shelf braces. Cut out with jigsaw; sand edges.

9 Referring to Fig. 3, notch bottom edges of bead board backing to accommodate side skirts for a flush fit.

TABLETOP

1 Place six 39½-inch 2x4s (A) on flat surface. Glue together and clamp to form center of tabletop; let dry.

2 Frame tabletop center with mitered 2x4s (B, C); glue and clamp. For additional strength, secure mitered corners together using 2½-inch screws. Let Dry.

BOTTOM SUPPORT UNIT

1 Place both left legs (D) on flat surface approximately 2 feet apart with notched edges facing up. Place two 25-inch 2x4 braces (E) into notches with edges flush; secure with glue and screws. Repeat for right legs.

2 For bottom cleats, use ³/₁₆-inch bit to drill 17 pilot holes in each

21¾-inch 2x2 (F), as shown in Fig. 4. Place left and right leg sections on flat surface with braces (E) facing down. Place cleats inside leg pieces with tops of cleats (F) flush with tops of braces (E). Attach bottom cleats to braces with glue and five exterior screws.

3 For bottom shelf, invert right and left leg sections and place on flat surface approximately 4 feet apart. Glue and clamp ends of six 46½-inch 2x4s (G) to braces and cleats evenly spaced. Using 2 screws per end, attach through bottom of cleats (Fig. 4).

4 Referring to Fig. 5 for placement, predrill four ³/₁₆-inch holes in each of the four 4-inch 2x2s (H) for top cleats. Using two 2½-inch exterior screws and glue, attach to inside edge of each leg between top brace and side skirt.

PROJECT SIZE
49x54x26¼ inches

TOOLS
- Circular saw or table saw
- Miter saw
- Jigsaw or scroll saw
- Router and round over bit
- Clamps, general and for mitered corners
- Mechanics square
- Drill bits sized to fit exterior screws
- ³/₁₆-inch drill bit
- Counter sink bit

SUPPLIES
- 2x6 framing studs: 10 feet
- 2x4 framing studs: 62 feet
- 2x2 framing studs: 6 feet
- Poplar 1x6: 28 feet
- 8-foot-long poplar 1x6 planed to ½-inch thickness
- 48-inch-wide x 24-inch-high ⅜-inch bead board
- Dust mask
- Safety glasses
- 80- and 150-grit sandpaper
- 1¼-, 2½-inch exterior screws
- Exterior glue
- 1- and 2-inch exterior finish nails
- Wood putty
- Green acrylic paint
- Exterior stain or paint

SHELF UNIT

1 Using finish nails throughout, attach top back (I) to top shelf (J) from underside of shelf.

2 Attach shelf skirt (K) to front edge of middle shelf (L). Attach sides (M) to top shelf; attach middle shelf to sides 12 inches from bottom.

ASSEMBLE & FINISH

1 Anchor tabletop to leg supports with side and front edges flush, using two 2½-inch screws through each top cleat (H). **Note:** *There should be a ⅜-inch gap at back to accommodate bead board backing.*

2 For skirt, anchor two 25-inch 1x6s (N) to sides of tabletop with exterior finish nails or screws. Attach one 48-inch 1x6 (O) to front of tabletop in same manner.

3 Place shelf unit on tabletop. Attach notched bead board backing to shelf unit through predrilled holes using 1¼-inch screws (Fig. 3).

4 Secure shelve unit to table by screwing shelf braces (P) to table from bottom, then screwing shelf sides to braces (Fig. 6).

5 Following manufacturer's directions, fill and sand exposed screw and nail holes with wood putty.

6 Paint ivy cutouts with green acrylic paint; let dry. Paint table/

shelf unit with exterior stain or paint; let dry.

7 Using 1-inch finish nails, attach ivy cutouts to skirt front and sides, shelf skirt and top back as shown in photo. Fill and sand nail holes with wood putty, then retouch paint. ✳

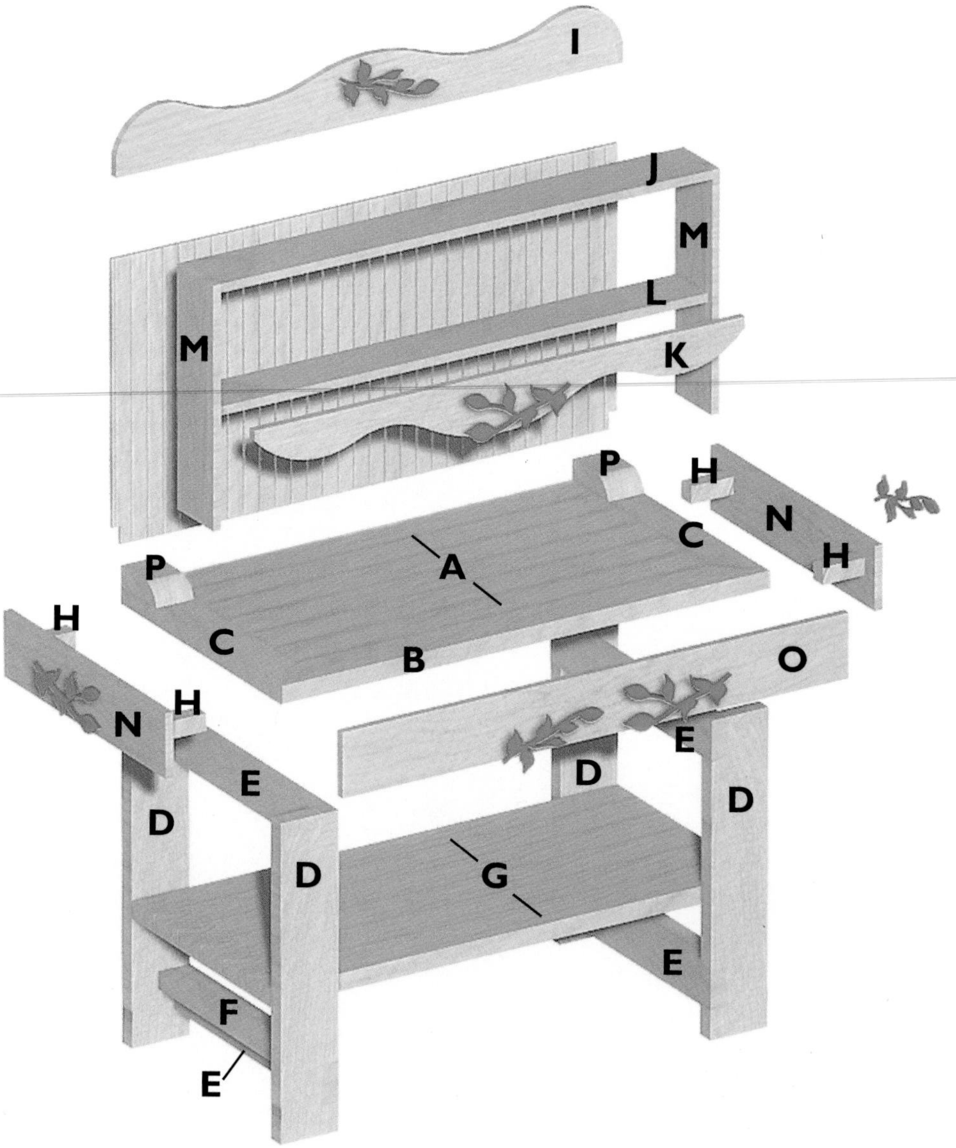

IVY POTTING TABLE CUTTING CHART

P	T	W	L	#
A	2"	4"	39½"	6
B	2"	4"	46½"	1
C	2"	4"	25⅝"	2
D	2"	6"	27"	4
E	2"	4"	25"	4
F	2"	2"	21¾"	2
G	2"	4"	46½"	6
H	2"	2"	4"	4
I	1"	6"	48"	1
J	1"	6"	46½"	1
K	1"	6"	46½"	1
L	1"	6"	46½"	1
M	1"	6"	20½"	2
N	1"	6"	25"	2
O	1"	6"	48"	1
P	2"	4"	5½"	2

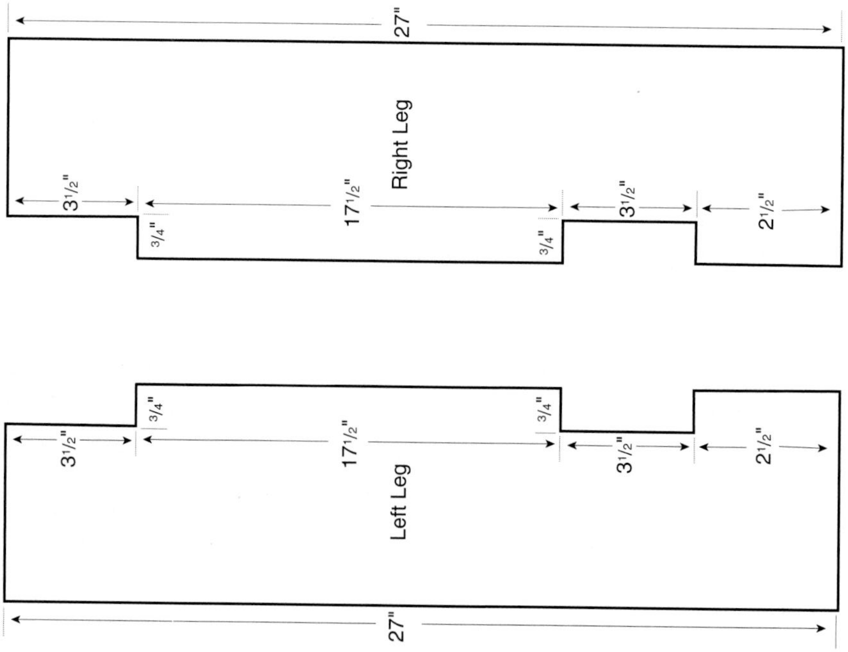

Ivy Potting Table
Fig. 1

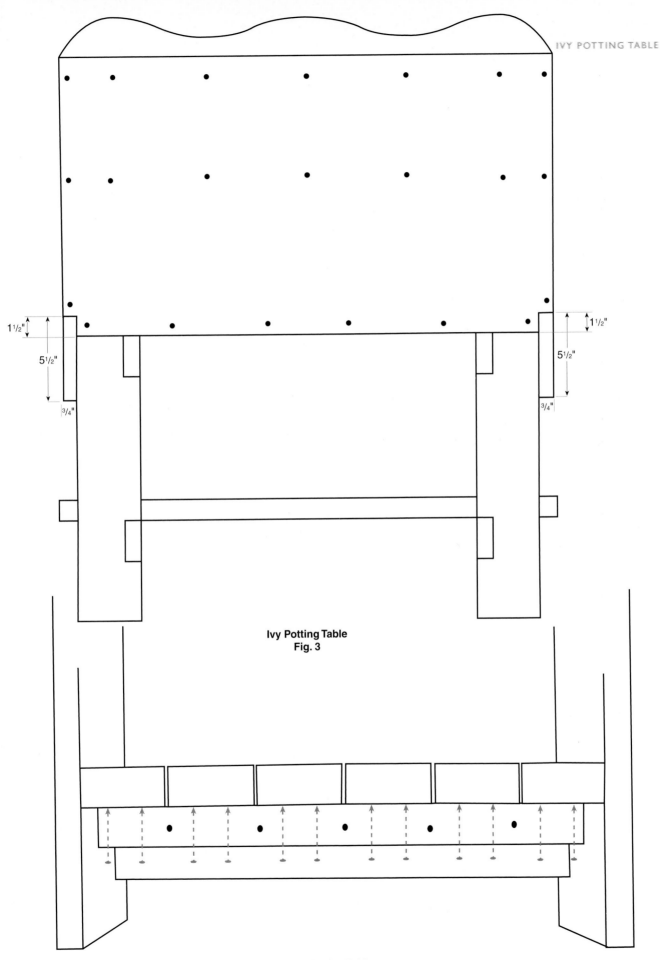

1 1/2"

1 1/2"

5 1/2"

5 1/2"

3/4"

3/4"

Ivy Potting Table
Fig. 3

Ivy Potting Table
Fig. 4

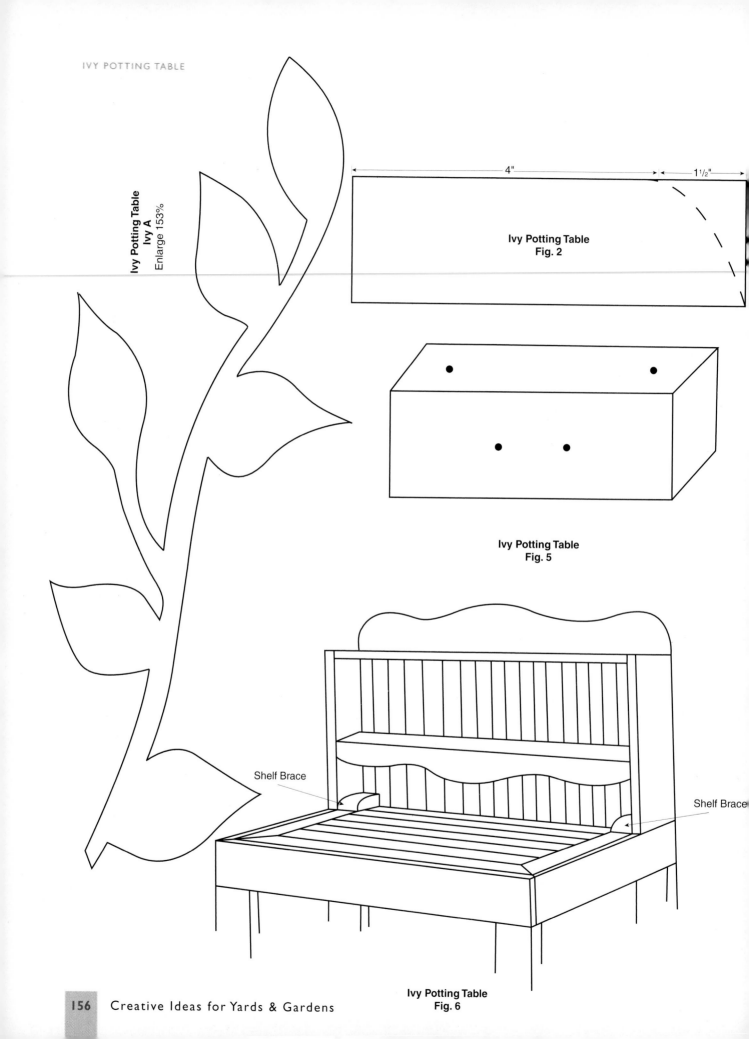

Ivy Potting Table
Ivy A
Enlarge 153%

4"   1½"

Ivy Potting Table
Fig. 2

Ivy Potting Table
Fig. 5

Shelf Brace

Shelf Brace

Ivy Potting Table
Fig. 6

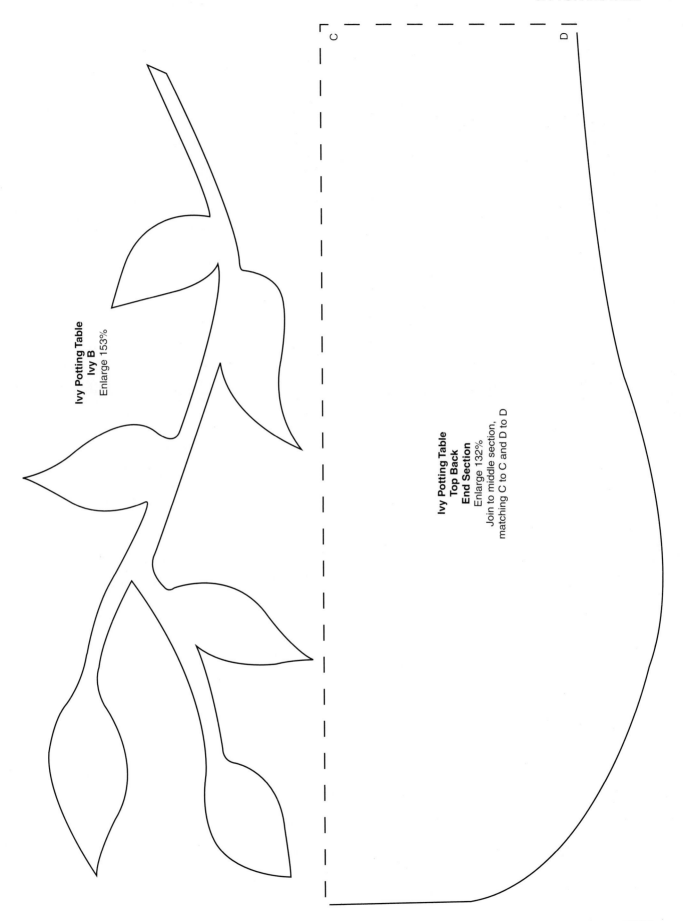

Ivy Potting Table
Ivy B
Enlarge 153%

C

D

Ivy Potting Table
Top Back
End Section
Enlarge 132%
Join to middle section,
matching C to C and D to D

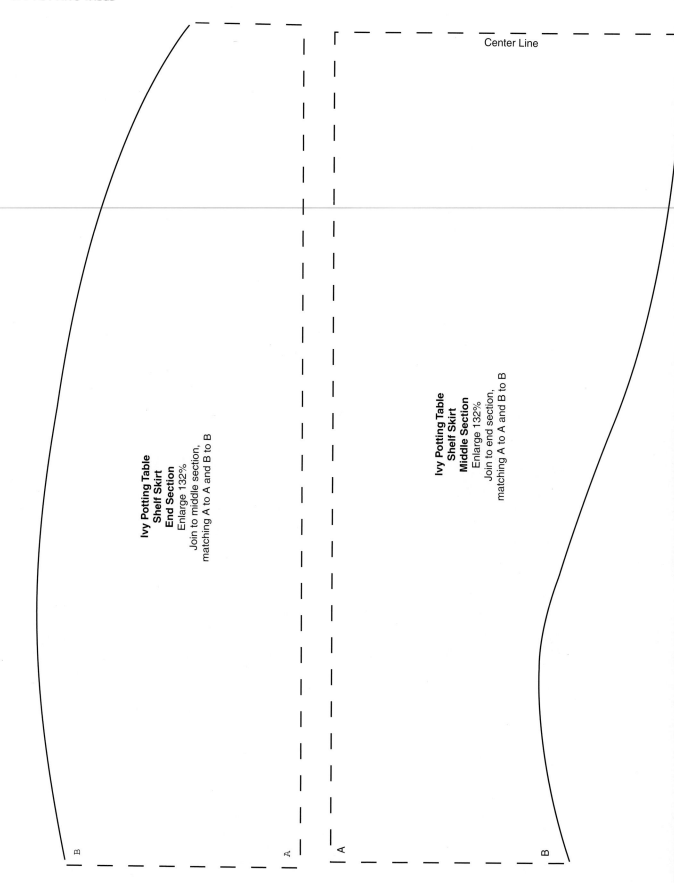

Center Line

Ivy Potting Table
Shelf Skirt
End Section
Enlarge 132%
Join to middle section,
matching A to A and B to B

Ivy Potting Table
Shelf Skirt
Middle Section
Enlarge 132%
Join to end section,
matching A to A and B to B

B

A

A

B

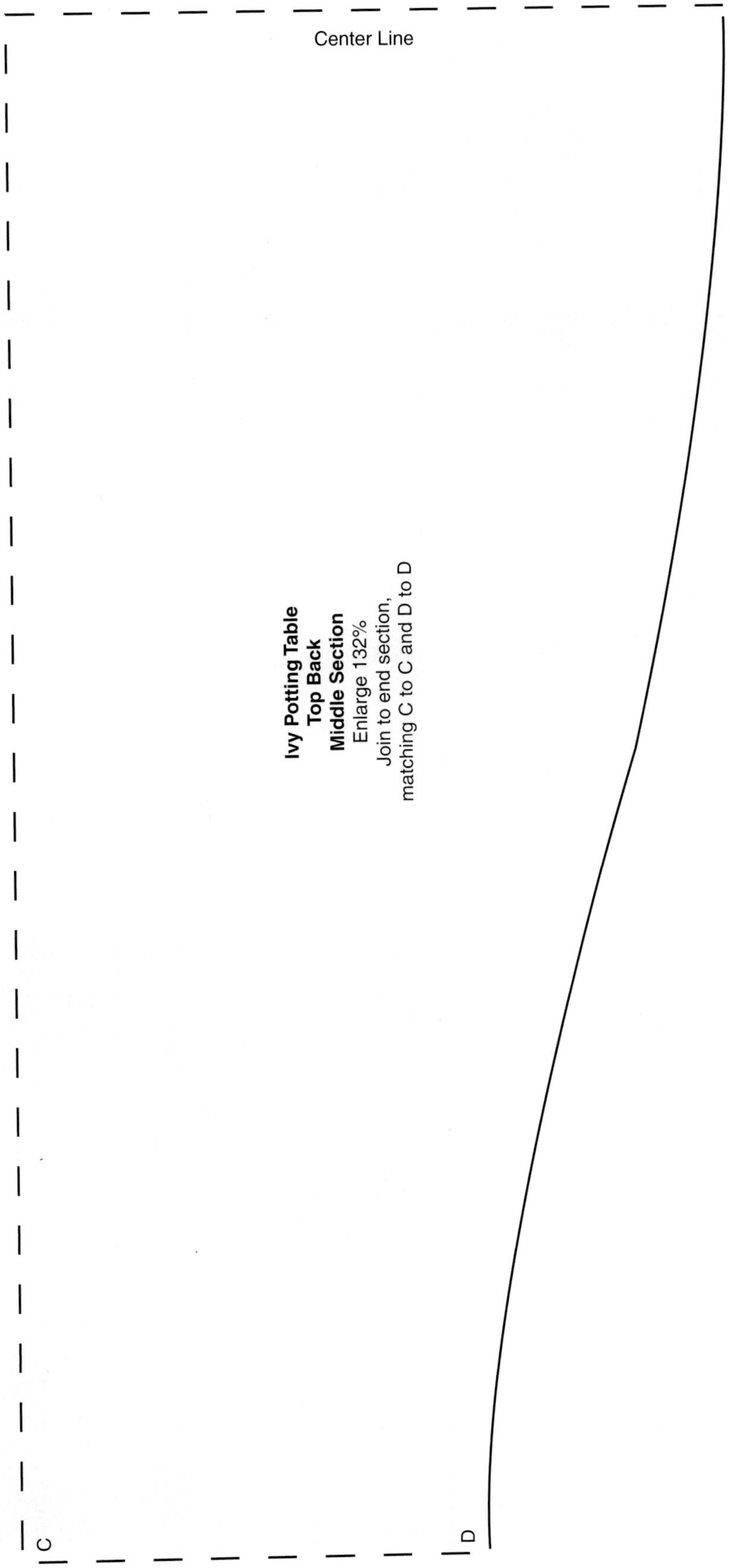

Center Line

Ivy Potting Table
Top Back
Middle Section
Enlarge 132%
Join to end section,
matching C to C and D to D

C

D

FLOWERPOT SHELF

Design by Cindy Reusser

This is a great project for people who want to create their own garden on a balcony or in their apartment. This easy-to-make project was made from pine, but teak or cedar would also work nicely.

CUTTING

1 Cut 1x12 into one 34½-inch length (A).

2 Cut 1x8 into one 34½-inch length (B) and two 7¼-inch lengths (C).

3 Cut 1x2 into one 34½-inch length (D).

4 For back, mark 7¼ inches from bottom edge on each end of 34½-inch 1x12 (A); lightly mark a vertical line across width of same board at center point (17¼ inches from each end). Tie 40-inch length of string to pencil. With pencil at center top of board, hold end of string at a point 30 inches below center bottom of board. Referring to Fig. 1, draw line for arch. Drill a ¾-inch hole at center top 1½ inches below edge. Cut along line to produce arch. Sand as necessary.

5 For bottom, mark locations for holes on 34½-inch 1x8 (B) as indicated in Fig. 2. Cut three 5¾-inch holes. Sand as necessary.

6 Trace side bracket pattern onto each 7¼-inch 1x8 (C). Cut out and sand rough edges.

ASSEMBLE & FINISH

1 Assemble back, side brackets and bottom with galvanized 2-inch drywall screws. Use approximately eight 5 penny nails to attach 34½-inch 1x2 (D) across front edge of bottom.

2 Fill all visible nail holes with wood putty, and sand, following manufacturer's directions.

3 Sand entire piece. Apply primer and paint following manufacturer's directions.

4 Attach 35# D hangers to back. Hang shelf; place flowerpots in holes. ✾

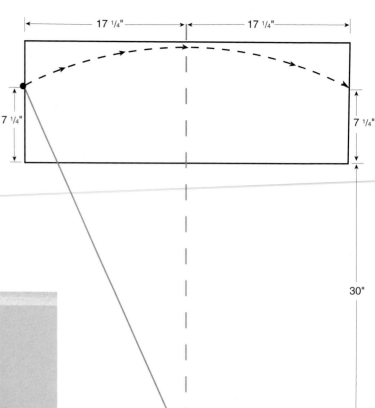

**Flowerpot Shelf
Fig. 1**

PROJECT SIZE
34½x8¾x11 inches

TOOLS
• Table saw or circular saw
• Band saw, 20-inch scroll saw, or jigsaw
• Drill with adjustable circle-cutting drill bit, or jigsaw

SUPPLIES
• 1x12: one 3-foot length
• 1x8: one 5-foot length
• 1x2: one 3-foot length
• 40 inches string
• Pencil
• Sandpaper
• Eight 2-inch galvanized drywall screws
• Eight 5 penny nails
• Wood putty
• Exterior wood primer and paint
• Two 35# rated D hangers
• Three 6-inch flower pots

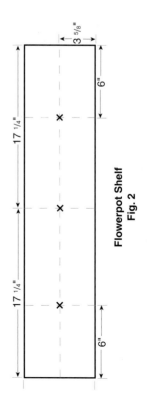

**Flowerpot Shelf
Fig. 2**

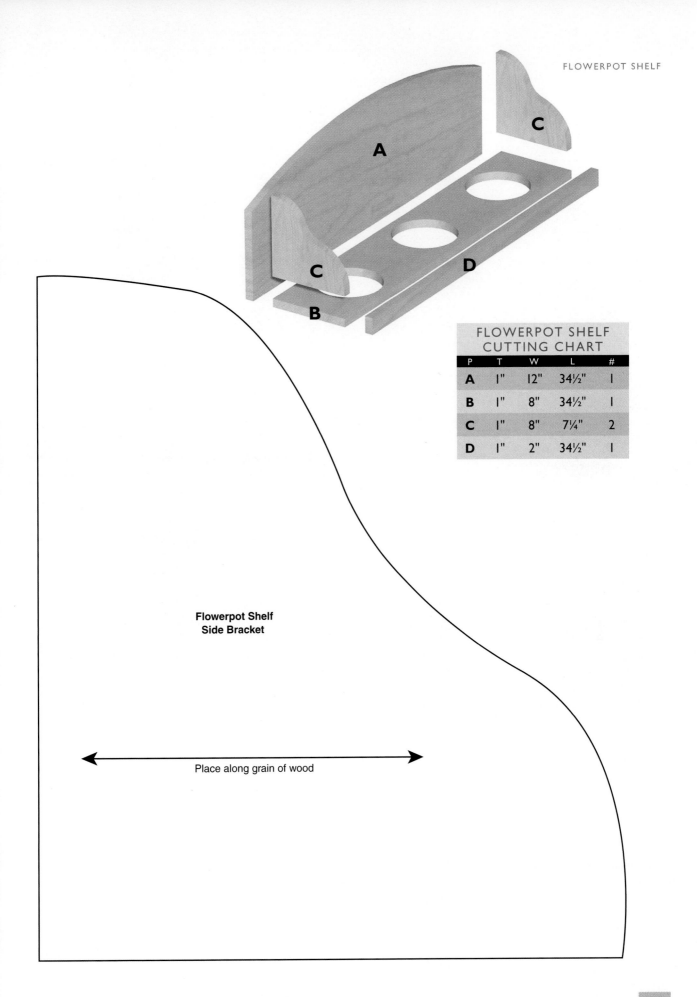

**FLOWERPOT SHELF
CUTTING CHART**

P	T	W	L	#
A	1"	12"	34½"	1
B	1"	8"	34½"	1
C	1"	8"	7¼"	2
D	1"	2"	34½"	1

**Flowerpot Shelf
Side Bracket**

← Place along grain of wood →

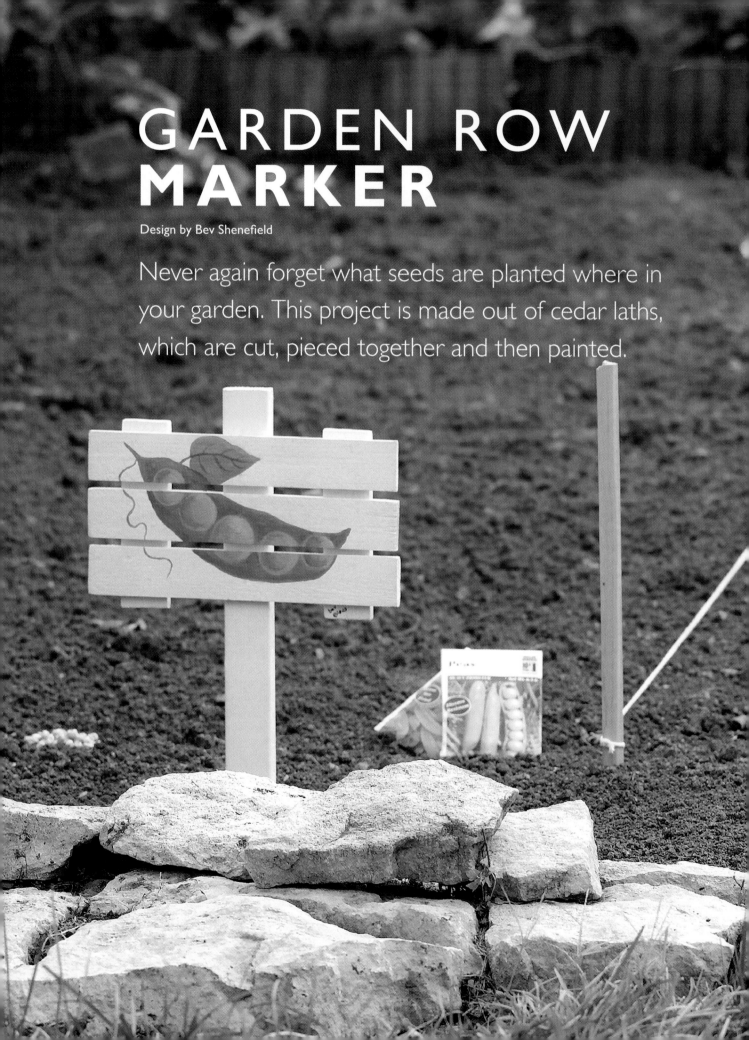

GARDEN ROW MARKER

Design by Bev Shenefield

Never again forget what seeds are planted where in your garden. This project is made out of cedar laths, which are cut, pieced together and then painted.

CUTTING

1 Use handsaw to cut cedar lath into three 10-inch lengths and two 6-inch lengths.

2 Sand laths and stake as needed; wipe clean with tack cloth.

PAINTING

1 Paint laths and stake with two or three coats soft white, letting dry after each coat.

ASSEMBLE & FINISH

1 Referring to assembly diagram, use ¾-inch nails to nail 10-inch laths across 6-inch laths.

2 Center assembled laths on stake 1½ inches from top of stake. Nail in place using 1-inch nails. Touch up all nails with soft white.

3 Use graphite paper to transfer pattern to front of laths. Paint pod Hauser medium green, leaf and tendril jade green, and peas with Hauser light green; shade with jade green. Let dry. Paint stem and veins on leaf with Hauser medium green; let dry.

4 Apply satin varnish to front of laths; let dry. ❀

PROJECT SIZE
10x15½ inches

TOOLS
• Handsaw

SUPPLIES
• 48 inches cedar lath
• 15-inch surveyor stake
• Fine-grit sandpaper
• Tack cloth
• Soft white #DSA02 Americana Satins acrylic paint from DecoArt
• Paintbrushes
• Small nails: ¾-inch and 1-inch
• Graphite paper
• Americana acrylic paint from DecoArt: Hauser light green #DA131, jade green #DA57 and Hauser medium green #DA132
• Satin varnish

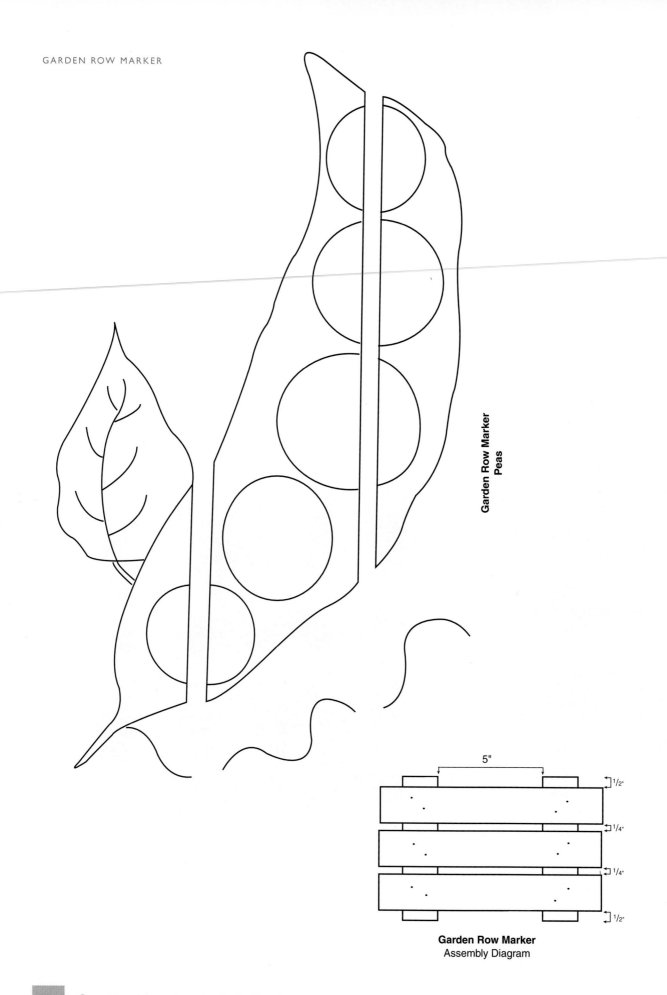

Garden Row Marker
Peas

5"

1/2"

1/4"

1/4"

1/2"

Garden Row Marker
Assembly Diagram

FLOWER BED MARKER

Design by Bev Shenefield

No artistic skill is required to create this quick-and-easy project. It will add an extra-special touch to your garden and mark where you planted each row!

PROJECT SIZE
4x14½x⅜ inches

SUPPLIES
- 4x14½x⅜-inch wooden picket
- Soft white #DSA02 Americana Satins acrylic paint from DecoArt
- Paintbrushes
- Brown paper bag
- Front of seed packet
- Exterior decoupage liquid
- Satin varnish
- Fine-point black permanent marker

PAINTING

1 Paint all sides of picket with soft white; let dry.

2 Rub painted surface with piece of brown paper bag to smooth. Apply a second coat of soft white; let dry.

ASSEMBLE & FINISH

1 Following manufacturer's directions, apply exterior decoupage liquid to wrong side of seed packet front; press onto upper portion of picket centered between sides.

2 Smooth out wrinkles and apply two additional coats of decoupage liquid as directed by manufacturer. Let dry.

3 Varnish all sides of picket with one coat of satin varnish; let dry.

4 Using fine-point black permanent marker, outline seed packet with double lines, overlapping at corners. ✳

GARDEN HOSE GUIDE

Design by Bonnie Dunnewind

Protect your lovely flowers from the hose when you place this decorative woodburned sign on the edge of your flower garden.

PROJECT NOTES

Follow manufacturer's safety instructions when using woodburner.

Practice making slow small sketching strokes on a scrap piece of pine before burning designs. Do not use pressure; the slower you go the darker the strokes will be.

Occasionally clean woodburner tip as you work by dragging it across fine-grit sandpaper.

INSTRUCTIONS

1 Transfer design onto basswood plaque using graphite paper.

2 Set woodburner to low setting. Using calligraphy point, begin burning letters; burn several times to achieve desired effects. Allow woodburner to cool. Change to the pointed tip. Burn in flowers and leaves.

3 Using photo as a guide, color design with oil color pencils as follows:

Flowers
are
Mother
Nature's
Perfume

Flower petals—base coat with white; repeat using lemon yellow over the white; shade with violet and yellow.

Flower center—base coat with sienna brown; highlight with orange or yellow orange.

Leaves—base coat with lemon yellow; shade edges with medium green and green; shade next to the center line of leaves with blue green.

4 Drive several long nails into scrap piece of wood. Place plaque on protruding nails; seal with two light coats of spray acrylic sealer, following manufacturer's directions. Let dry overnight.

5 Following manufacturer's directions, apply three coats of exterior/interior clear finish on all sides, letting dry between coats and sanding lightly after first two coats.

6 On back of plaque, place copper straps 6-inches apart over copper pipe; mark location of screws with awl. Attach straps and pipe to plaque with metal screws.

7 To use, pound copper pipe into flower garden edge, leaving approximately 5 inches of tubing exposed to catch garden hose. ✱

SUPPLIES
- 5x11x⅜-inch basswood plaque
- Graphite paper
- Woodburning tool with calligraphy point 6-B (⅛-inch) and angle blade tip 1A or 1B
- Oil color pencils from Walnut Hollow: white #9007, lemon yellow #1411, yellow #9001, yellow orange #9014, sienna brown #1418, orange #9004, green #9006, medium green #1410, blue green #9018, violet #9032
- Scrap piece of wood and several long nails
- Spray acrylic sealer
- Satin Helmsman Spar Urethane exterior/interior clear finish from Minwax
- Fine-grit sandpaper
- Two ½-inch copper straps
- 20 inches ½-inch copper pipe
- Awl
- Four ⅜-inch #8 stainless steel metal screws

Flowers are Mother Nature's Perfume

# CONVERSION CHARTS

Standard Lumber Dimensions

NOMINAL	ACTUAL	METRIC
1" x 2"	¾" x 1½"	19 x 38 mm
1" x 3"	¾" x 2½"	19 x 64 mm
1" x 4"	¾" x 3½"	19 x 89 mm
1" x 5"	¾" x 4½"	19 x 114 mm
1" x 6"	¾" x 5½"	19 x 140 mm
1" x 7"	¾" x 6¼"	19 x 159 mm
1" x 8"	¾" x 7¼"	19 x 184 mm
1" x 10"	¾" x 9¼"	19 x 235 mm
1" x 12"	¾" x 11¼"	19 x 286 mm
1¼" x 4"	1" x 3½"	25 x 89 mm
1¼" x 6"	1" x 5½"	25 x 140 mm
1¼" x 8"	1" x 7¼"	25 x 184 mm
1¼" x 10"	1" x 9¼"	25 x 235 mm
1¼" x 12"	1" x 11¼"	25 x 286 mm
1½" x 4"	1¼" x 3½"	32 x 89 mm
1½" x 6"	1¼" x 5½"	32 x 140 mm
1½" x 8"	1¼" x 7¼"	32 x 184 mm
1½" x 10"	1¼" x 9¼"	32 x 235 mm
1½" x 12"	1¼" x 11¼"	32 x 286 mm
2" x 3"	1½" x 2½"	38 x 64 mm
2" x 4"	1½" x 3½"	38 x 89 mm
2" x 6"	1½" x 5½"	38 x 140 mm
2" x 8"	1½" x 7¼"	38 x 184 mm
2" x 10"	1½" x 9¼"	38 x 235 mm
2" x 12"	1½" x 11¼"	38 x 286 mm
3" x 6"	2½" x 5½"	64 x 140 mm
4" x 4"	3½" x 3½"	89 x 89 mm
4" x 6"	3½" x 5½"	89 x 140 mm

Metric Conversions

U.S. MEASUREMENT		MULTIPLIED BY		METRIC MEASUREMENT
Yards	x	.9144	=	Meters (M)
Yards	x	91.44	=	Centimeters (CM)
Inches	x	2.54	=	Centimeters (CM
Inches	x	25.40	=	Millimeters (MM)
Inches	x	.0254	=	Meters (M)
METRIC MEASUREMENT		MULTIPLIED BY METRIC MEASUREMENT		
Centimeters	x	.3937	=	Inches
Meters	x	1.0936	=	Yards

Metric Equivalency Chart

MM = Millimeters CM = Centimeters

Inches to Millimeters and Centimeters

INCHES	MM	CM	INCHES	CM	INCHES	CM
1/8	3	0.3	9	22.9	30	76.2
1/4	6	0.6	10	25.4	31	78.7
3/8	10	1.0	11	27.9	32	81.3
1/2	13	1.3	12	30.5	33	83.8
5/8	16	1.6	13	33.0	34	86.4
3/4	19	1.9	14	35.6	35	88.9
7/8	22	2.2	15	38.1	36	91.4
1	25	2.5	16	40.6	37	94.0
1 1/4	32	3.2	17	43.2	38	96.5
1 1/2	38	3.8	18	45.7	39	99.1
1 3/4	44	4.4	19	48.3	40	101.6
2	51	5.1	20	50.8	41	104.1
2 1/2	64	6.4	21	53.3	42	106.7
3	76	7.6	22	55.9	43	109.2
3 1/2	89	8.9	23	58.4	44	111.8
4	102	10.2	24	61.0	45	114.3
4 1/2	114	11.4	25	63.5	46	116.8
5	127	12.7	26	66.0	47	119.4
6	152	15.2	27	68.6	48	121.9
7	178	17.8	28	71.1	49	124.5
8	203	20.3	29	73.7	50	127.0

Yards to Meters

YARDS	METERS	YARDS	METERS	YARDS	METERS	YARDS	METERS	YARDS	METERS
1/8	0.11	2 1/8	1.94	4 1/8	3.77	6 1/8	5.60	8 1/8	7.43
1/4	0.23	2 1/4	2.06	4 1/4	3.89	6 1/4	5.72	8 1/4	7.54
3/8	0.34	2 3/8	2.17	4 3/8	4.00	6 3/8	5.83	8 3/8	7.66
1/2	0.46	2 1/2	2.29	4 1/2	4.11	6 1/2	5.94	8 1/2	7.77
5/8	0.57	2 5/8	2.40	4 5/8	4.23	6 5/8	6.06	8 5/8	7.89
3/4	0.69	2 3/4	2.51	4 3/4	4.34	6 3/4	6.17	8 3/4	8.00
7/8	0.80	2 7/8	2.63	4 7/8	4.46	6 7/8	6.29	8 7/8	8.12
1	0.91	3	2.74	5	4.57	7	6.40	9	8.23
1 1/8	1.03	3 1/8	2.86	5 1/8	4.69	7 1/8	6.52	9 1/8	8.34
1 1/4	1.14	3 1/4	2.97	5 1/4	4.80	7 1/4	6.63	9 1/4	8.46
1 3/8	1.26	3 3/8	3.09	5 3/8	4.91	7 3/8	6.74	9 3/8	8.57
1 1/2	1.37	3 1/2	3.20	5 1/2	5.03	7 1/2	6.86	9 1/2	8.69
1 5/8	1.49	3 5/8	3.31	5 5/8	5.14	7 5/8	6.97	9 5/8	8.80
1 3/4	1.60	3 3/4	3.43	5 3/4	5.26	7 3/4	7.09	9 3/4	8.92
1 7/8	1.71	3 7/8	3.54	5 7/8	5.37	7 7/8	7.20	9 7/8	9.03
2	1.83	4	3.66	6	5.49	8	7.32	10	9.14

A NOTE ON SAFETY

By Sarah Miller

As with any hobby that involves power tools and sharp blades, woodworking requires that safety be your primary focus.

I used to find people who wore safety goggles (even if just *thinking* about woodworking) a bit silly, and then one day I was using a screwdriver to put a screw into the underside of a countertop. I hadn't drilled the hole big enough, so I started to exert force on the screw. At that point, the screwdriver slipped out of the screw's slot and went right into my eye, cutting my contact lens in half and putting a half-inch slice on my eyeball.

Everything worked out fine thanks to the city's eye hospital, but I think you understand the important lesson I learned. In a flash, something very bad can happen with the most innocent-looking tools. That moment changed my whole outlook on safety, and I hope yours, too.

A few guidelines to think about and follow:

Cover up. Always wear ANSI-rated (American National Standards Institute Inc.) eyewear, and hearing protection. Eyes and ears are tough to replace. Power tools are louder than you think, and will take their toll on your ears if you let them.

If it can cut, drill or alter wood or metal, it can do the same to you, too. Know where you are in relation to your tools and their cutting path. Also be aware if you are in the direct line of a tool should it slip, kick, or throw the material you're working on.

If it spins, imagine yourself spinning along with it. Tools that spin can grab anything that gets in their way. You don't want your drill or router to catch your hair or bracelet. Remove all loose jewelry, secure your hair, and make sure that everything that you're wearing is tight-fitting and secure.

Never use more power, blade, or machine than you need. When you are cutting, only expose the amount of blade you need. If you need to cut something that is small, use a small saw. Don't buy a 5hp table saw, when you will only need a 2hp saw. Don't expose yourself to needless harm, and "always use the right tool for the job."

Just because they are just watching, doesn't mean they can't get hurt. Make sure that everyone (including your pet) is clear when you are working on a project. Tools can throw your working material quite a distance.

Safety equipment was invented for a reason. There is *never* a reason to have your fingers near a saw blade. Always use a pushstick, pushblocks, or whatever other item is appropriate. If you are drilling, put the wood in a vice, don't just hold it in your hand. If you are sawing, use sawhorses, not your lap. And just because you are using safety equipment, don't think that you can get sloppy. Accidents are just that—accidents.

If you can't devote your full attention to what you're doing, don't do it. You don't want to be startled or distracted when you are using power equipment or sharp tools. When you are concentrating, you don't want to be surprised by a cell phone vibrating in your pocket, or a child pulling on your pants leg.

Anticipate what will happen next, yet expect surprises. If you are sawing wood, think about where it will fall. If you are drilling a hole, know what's behind your piece of wood. And always make sure that your project is supported well, and securely. Also, make sure that your body is well-positioned should your saw kick back, or sawhorse fall down.

Keep a clean, organized work area so that you can move about easily and safely. Keep extension cords out of the way or taped down securely. Make a place for all of your tools and supplies. Keep lumber, boards and other supplies stacked neatly so that you don't stumble forward or backward over them. Frequently pick up your work area so that you don't damage your work in progress or injure yourself.

If it feels dangerous, it probably is. People were born with a sixth sense, which is the one that detects danger. Unfortunately, more often than not, we ignore it. If you are about to do something that makes you think twice, stop. Don't be lazy or foolish when it comes to safety.

Don't rush. Woodworking is fun, so take your time. Rushing can make you careless.

Enjoy! If you follow safety rules, your career as a woman woodworker should be long and without incident. Now go have fun! ■

SPECIAL THANKS

We would like to thank Cindy and Neal Reusser and the staff of CR Designs for the help they provided throughout the publishing process. We also appreciate the help of Sandi Hauanio and Dana Van Pelt. We thank the talented woodworking designers whose work is featured in this collection.

Mary Ayres
Flower Press, 85

Bonnie Dunnewind
Garden Hose Guide, 168

Rue Ann Flanders
Berry Branch
  Decorative Fence, 95
Daisy Bench, 101
Ivy Potting Table, 150
Tree Earrings, 122
Tulip Decorative Fence, 92

Barbara Greve
Stencil in Relief
  Garden Sign, 142
How to Stencil
  in Relief, 144
Porch Railing Shelf, 22
Shabby-Chic-Syle Scroll
  Thermometer, 88
Small Wood Box, 36

Sandi Hauanio
Log Cabin
  Steppingstone, 135

Peek-A-Boo
  Steppingstones, 138
Painted Garden Table, 145
Wooden
  Steppingstones, 132

Johanna Johanson.
Firewood Box, 40
Southwestern-Style
  Bench, 106

Lisa Marto Weber
Bench Planter, 24
Flower Box, 56
Flower Blossom
  Luminaries, 110
Golden Star
  Wind Chimes, 127
Tile Tabletop, 15

Barbara Matthiessen
Grill Cart, 44
Reflections Planter, 58
Wood & Copper
  Wind Chimes, 33

Mary Nelson
Honeybees Feeder, 76
Sail Away
  Napkin Holders, 61

Cindy Reusser
Birdhouse Peg Rack, 18
Cat Birdhouse, 118
Flowerpot Shelf, 160
Mailbox, 28
Pineapple Welcome, 8
Serving Tray, 66
Welcome Plaque, 12

Bev Shenefield
Barbecue Caddy, 74
Birdhouse Fence, 98
Flower Bed Marker, 167
Garden Row Marker, 164
Potting Table, 124
Storage Bench, 50
Trivet Trio, 69